SWU-NAP- 018

UNIFORMS OF RUSSIAN ARMY DURING THE NAPOLEONIC WAR VOL.13

UNDER THE REIGN OF ALEXANDER I
EMPEROR OF RUSSIA BETWEEN 1801 AND 1825
CORPS OF ENGINEERS: SAPPERS, PIONEERS AND GARRISON

From the Viskovatov's greatest work:
"Historical description of the clothing and
arms of the Russian Army"

English translation by Mark Conrad

SOLDIERSHOP PUBLISHING

AUTHOR

Aleksandr Vasilevich Viskovatov born 22 April (4 May New Style) 1804, died 27 February (11 March) 1858 in St. Petersburg, Russian military historian. He graduated from the 1st Cadet Corps and served in the artillery, the hydrographic depot of the Naval Ministry, and then in the Department of Military Educational Institutions. He mainly studied historical artifacts and the histories of military units. Viskovatov's greatest work was the Historical Description of the Clothing and Arms of the Russian Army.

ACKNOWLEDGEMENTS

A Special Thanks to NYPL and other institutions for their kindly permission to use some images of his archives, collections or books used in our book.

Title: **UNIFORMS OF RUSSIAN ARMY DURING THE NAPOLEONIC WAR VOL. 13**
Corps of Engineers: Sappers, Pioneers and Garrison
By A.V.Viskovatov. Serie edit by Luca S. Cristini. First edition by Soldiershop. August 2017
Cover & Art Design: Luca S. Cristini. Plates re-colorations by Anna Cristini.
ISBN code: 978-88-93272643
Published by Soldiershop publishing, via Padre Davide, 7 - 24050 Zanica (BG) ITALY. www.soldiershop.com

UNIFORMS
OF THE RUSSIAN ARMY
DURING THE NAPOLEONIC
WAR VOL. 13

UNDER THE REIGN OF ALEXANDER I EMPEROR OF
RUSSIA BETWEEN 1801 AND 1825

*

CORPS OF ENGINEERS: SAPPERS, PIONEERS & GARRISON

NCO and soldier of Moscow Guards (1820 about)

HISTORICAL DESCRIPTION OF THE CLOTHING AND ARMS
OF THE RUSSIAN ARMY - A.V. VISKOVATOV
(First English translation by Mark Conrad)

Soldiershop is glad to presents the complete collection of the great job made by A.V. Viskovatov dedicated to the uniforms and weapons belonging to the Russian army during the Napoleonic period, until 1825. The time we considered corresponds to the reigns of two Tzars: Paul I, who reigned since 1769 until his murder on the 23rd of March 1801, and his son Aleksandr Pavlovič Romanov, that with the title of Alexander I, sat on the throne until the 1st December 1825.

Our reprint in based on the original 19th century volumes, to be precise the volumes from 7 to 9 are dedicated to the reign of Paul I; this first part is distributed on 7 volumes, having a numbering from 1 to 7. From number 10 to 18 of the original volumes, the second part is dedicated to the Russian troops under Alexander I. These still being worked on and they will be soon ready, distributed on twenty volumes approximately. Our new edition, the first ever published in English, both on paper and digital format, boasts a large number of color plates, many of them unpublished and coloured by our team of expert artists and scholars of uniformology. Each volume is based on 50/70 plates, always accompanied by the original translated text which describes the uniforms, the organization and the armament of the Russian army of the period.

A unique work in its genre, a must have in any respecting collection!

Aleksandr Vasilevich Viskovatov born 22 April (4 May New Style) 1804, died 27 February (11 March) 1858 in St. Petersburg, Russian military historian. He graduated from the 1st Cadet Corps and served in the artillery, the hydrographic depot of the Naval Ministry, and then in the Department of Military Educational Institutions.

He mainly studied historical artifacts and the histories of military units. Viskovatov's greatest work was the Historical Description of the Clothing and Arms of the Russian Army (Vols. 1-30, St. Petersburg, 1841-62; 2nd ed. Vols. 1-34, St. Petersburg - Novosibirsk - Leningrad, 1899-1948). This work is based on a great quantity of archival documents and contains four thousand colored illustrations.

Viskovatov was the author of Chronicles of the Russian Army (Books 1-20, St. Petersburg, 1834-42) and Chronicles of the Russian Imperial Army (Parts 1-7, St. Petersburg, 1852). He collected valuable material on the history of the Russian navy which went into A Short Overview of Russian Naval Campaigns and General Voyages to the End of the XVII Century (St. Petersburg, 1864; 2nd edition Moscow, 1946). Together with A.I. Mikhailovskii-Danilevskii he helped prepare and create the Military Gallery in the Winter Palace.

He wrote the historical military inscriptions for the walls of the Hall of St. George in the Great Palace of the Kremlin. (From the article in the Soviet Military Encyclopedia.)

CONTENTS

*

RUSSIAN ARMY- ARTILLERY: FOOT, HORSE AND GARRISON ARTILLERY

CHANGES IN THE CLOTHING AND ARMAMENTS OF ARMY AND GARRISON ARTILLERY, ARMY SAPPERS AND PIONEERS, FIELD AND GARRISON ENGINEERS, MILITARY LABOR BATTALIONS AND COMPANIES, HIS IMPERIAL MAJESTY'S SUITE FOR QUARTERMASTER AFFAIRS, AND TOPOGRAPHERS, FROM 1801 THROUGH 1825:

XI. Army Sappers and Pioneers.
XII. Army Horse Pioneers.
XIII. Field and Garrison Engineers.
XIV. Military-Labor battalions and companies.
XV. HIS IMPERIAL MAJESTY's Suite for Quartermaster Affairs.
XVI. Topographers.
Source notes.

INVALID COMPANIES AND COMMANDS

4 January 1804– One *Invalid company [Invalidnaya rota]* was established for each of the Garrison battalions: Minsk, Yekaterinoslavl, Vologda, Velikii-Ustyug, Ufa, and Vyatka (310).

14 April 1804– Five *Invalid companies* were established for the Aleksandrovsk Manufactory [*Aleksandrovskaya manufaktura*] (in St. Petersburg) (311).

22 August 1804– An *Invalid company* was established for the Riga Garrison Regiment (312).

12 September 1804– From invalids of the Court Department [*Pridvornoe vedomstvo*] who were at Gatchina and Pavlovsk for the palaces and gardens, there were established one *Pavlovsk* and two *Gatchina Invalid Companies*.

After this, the distribution of all Invalid companies was as follows: in Gatchina – 2, in Pavlovsk – 1, at the Aleksandrovsk Manufactory – 5, with the Moscow Garrison Regiment – 8, with the Astrakhan Regiment – 3, with the Dimitrievsk, Kizlyar, and Tobolsk regiments – 2 each, and 1 each with the Kazan and Irkutsk regiments and the Novgorod, Pskov, Smolensk, Minsk, Yekaterinoslavl, Vitebsk, Mogilev, Voronezh, Saratov, Tambov, Vladimir, Nizhnii-Novgorod, Tver, Penza, Vologda, Velikii-Ustyug, Tsaritsyn, Azov, Taganrog, Simbirsk, Ufa, Vyatka, Mozdok, Pernau, Arensburg, Biisk, Kizilsk, Verkhne-Uralsk, Troitsk, Zverinogolovsk, Orsk, Omsk, Petrovsk, Semipalatinsk, Zhelezinka, and Tomsk battalions, as well as in Stavropol, Bakhmut, Sudak, the Aleksandrovsk and Petrovsk fortresses, Yelisavetgrad (assigned to the Yekaterinoslavl Battalion), Staryi-Bykhov (assigned to the Mogilev Battalion), and Polotsk (assigned to the Vitebsk Battalion).

One Invalid command [*Invalidnaya komanda*] each was in St. Petersburg and Dünaburg and with the Viborg and Selenginsk Garrison Regiments, and there were also commands of Non-serving invalids [*Nesluzhashchie invalidy*] distributed in towns, established in 1764 and listed above in the overview of forces at the time of Emperor Alexander I's ascension to the throne (313).

21 January 1809– One *Invalid company* was established for the Oranienbaum and Peterhof palaces and gardens (314).

6 April 1809– An *Invalid company* was established for the Sestroretsk Arms Factory [*Sestroretskii Oruzheinyi zavod*] (315).

6 May 1809– One *Invalid company* each was established for the Viborg Garrison Regiment and the Fredrikshamn and Kexholm Garrison Battalions (316).

30 November 1809– An *Invalid company* was established in Narva for the garrison there (317).

5 January 1810– One *Invalid company* was established in the town of Vasa [*Vaza*] and two in Schlüsselburg (318).

26 October 1810– The Invalid company left in Minsk after the transfer of the Garrison battalion there to Bobruisk (23 August, 1810) was ordered to be called the *Minsk Invalid Company* (319).

27 March 1811– In general, all invalids of the Military Land Department [*Voenno-sukhoputnoe vedomstvo*, i.e. the Army – M.C.] were directed to be called *Military Invalids [Voennye invalidy]*, and along with this, they were divided into three classes [*razryady*]: *Mobile [Podvizhnye]*, *Serving [Sluzhashchie]*, and *Non-serving or Unfit [Nesluzhashchie ili Nesposobnye]*, and all these were used to form new *Invalid companies*, called *Mobile*, and new *Invalid commands*, called *District [Uezdnyi]* *commands.* Of the previous establishment there remained only two Invalid companies in Schlüsselburg, two with the Tobolsk Garrison Regiment, one with the Irkutsk, one in Narva, and one Invalid command each in St. Petersburg, with the Omsk and Selenginsk Garrison Regiments, and with the Petrovsk, Tomsk, Semipalatinsk, Omsk, Biisk, and Zhelezinka Garrison Battalions (320). At later times these companies and commands became:

31 March 1816– Narva company—joined the roster of Mobile Invalid companies, as №16 (321).

4 September 1816– The Tobolsk, Irkutsk, Omsk, Semipalatinsk, Biisk, and Zhelezinka battalions—became part of Mobile Invalid Companies №№75 and 76 and the District Invalid commands of Siberia Province, which were all established on this date (322).

21 November 1818– The St.-Petersburg command—joined Mobile Invalid Company №82, which was established on this date (323).

6 February 1819– The Schlüsselburg company—joined Mobile Invalid Company № 83 (324).

For an easier overview of the changes which they underwent, for the time after 27 March, 1811, all the Invalid companies and commands are treated in five classes: a.) *Mobile Invalid Companies*; b.) *Serving and Non-serving Invalid Commands*; c.) *Étape Invalid Commands*; and d.) *Salt Invalid Commands.*

a.) **Mobile Invalid Companies.**

27 March 1811– It was ordered to have 35 *Mobile Invalid companies [Podvizhniya Invalidniya roty]:* with the Guards regiments – 4, at Gatchina – 2, at Pavlovsk – 2, at Sveaborg – 1, for the Sestroretsk Arms Factory – 1, for the Tula Arms Factory – 1, for the Yekaterinoslavl Cloth Factory [*Yekaterinoslavskaya Sukonnaya fabrika*] – 1, for the Aleksandrovsk Manufactory – 4, for the Oranienbaum Hospital [*Oranienbaumskii gospital*] – 1, for the St.-Petersburg Commission of the Provisions Depot [*S.-Peterburgskaya Kommissiya Proviantskago Depo*] – 1, in St. Petersburg – 3, in New Finland [*Novaya Finlyandiya*] – 1, in Archangel – 1, in Moscow – 4, in Yekaterinoslavl – 1, in Yelisavetgrad – 4, in Astrakhan – 1, and in Kizlyar – 1 (325).

6 July 1811–To these companies were added another five: one—in Oranienbaum and Peterhof, for guarding Palace buildings and gardens; one—in Moscow, for the same purposes for the palaces and gardens there; one—for the 2nd Cadet Corps, for servants for the two Nobiliary battalions [*Dvoryanskie bataliony*] there; one—for the Pavlovsk Cloth Factory, and one—for the Izhevsk Arms Factory (326).

18 September 1811– Mobile Invalid companies were given numbers:

1 Companies with Guards regiments.
2 Ditto.
3 Ditto.
4 Ditto.
5 Companies with the 2nd Cadet Corps.
6 Ditto.
7 Company with the St.-Petersburg Commission of the Provisions Depot.
8 ——— at the Peterhof and Oranienbaum Palaces.
9 ——— at the Oranienbaum Hospital.
10 Companies at Gatchina.
11 Ditto.
12 Company at Pavlovsk.
13 Companies at the Aleksandrovsk Manufactory.
14 Ditto.
15 Ditto.
16 Ditto.
17 Company at the Sestroretsk Arms Factory.
18 ——— — Sveaborg.
19 ——— — the Moscow Palaces.
20 ——— — the Tula Arms Factory.
21 ——— — the Pavlovsk Cloth Factory.
22 ——— — Yekaterinoslavl Cloth Factory.
23 ——— — Izhevsk Arms Factory.
24 ——— — the field hospital in Kuopio.
25 ——— — — —— —— — Viborg.
26 ——— with the forces in Friedrichstadt [*Fridrikhshtadt*].

27 ——— — — ———— — Dünaburg.

28 ——— — — ———— — Sventsyany [*Sventsieny*].

29 ——— — — ———— — Drissa.

30 ——— — — ———— — Disna.

31 ——— — — ———— — Sebezh.

32 ——— — — ———— — Nesvizh.

33 ——— — — ———— — Novograd-Volynskii.

34 ——— — — ———— — Chernobyl.

35 ——— — — ———— — Kiev.

36 ——— — — ———— — Konevo.

37 ——— — — ———— — Sosnitsa.

38 ——— — — ———— — Jassy [*Yassy*].

39 ——— — — ———— — Bendery.

40 ——— — — ———— — Georgievsk.

41 ——— — — ———— — Tiflis [327].

15 October 1811– Four more Mobile Invalid companies were formed: *N*°*N*°*42, 43, 44, and 45*, designated for guard duties with the quarantines in the New Russia Territory [328].

31 January 1812– The *46th* Mobile Invalid Company was established for the Commissariat and Provisions Commissions in the towns of Kryuki and Kremenchug [329].

31 March 1816– In addition to the 46 Mobile Invalid companies in existence since 1811 and 1812, it was ordered to form 25 more, and consequently all of them, new as well as old, were distributed as follows:

Company N°1, formerly 5 — with the 2nd Cadet Corps.

———— 2, ——— 6 — ditto.

———— 3, no former N° - ditto.

———— 4, formerly 7 - at the St.-Petersburg Provisions Commission.

———— 5, ——— 13—— Aleksandrovsk Manufactory.

———— 6, ——— 14—— ditto.

———— 7, ——— 15—— ditto.

———— 8, ——— 16—— ditto.

———— 9, ——— 17 —— Sestroretsk Arms Factory.

———— 10, ——— 19 —— Palace buildings in Moscow.

———— 11, ——— 20 —— Tula Arms Factory.

———— 12, ——— 21 —— Pavlovsk State Cloth Factory.

———— 13, ——— 22 —— Yekaterinoslavl State Cloth Factory.

———— 14, ——— 23 —— Izhevsk Arms Factory.

———— 15, ——— 46 with the Commissariat and Provisions Commissions—in Kryuki.

———— 16, Narva Garrison in Narva.

———— 17, formerly 5 —at the hospital of the 1st Infantry Corps.

———— 18, newly formed— ditto.

———— 19, newly formed — hospitals of the 14th and 5th Infantry Divisions, one half-company at each hospital.

———— 20, formerly 30 — hospitals: 6th Infantry Division – two-thirds of the company, and with the 1st Hussar Division – one-third.

———— 21, newly formed with the hospital of the 2nd Hussar Division.

———— 22, —— —— hospitals of the 4th and 28th Infantry Divisions, one half-company each.

———— 23, —— —— hospitals of the 25th Infantry Division and 1st Dragoon Division, one half-company each.

———— 24, formerly 35 —— hospital of the 3rd Infantry Corps.

———— 25, newly formed —— hospitals of the 7th and 24th Infantry Divisions, one half-company each.

———— 26, —— —— — — hospitals of the 27th Infantry Division and 2nd Hussar Division, one half-company each.

———— 27, formerly 28 —— hospital of the 4th Infantry Corps.

———— 28, newly formed —— hospitals of the 11th Infantry Division and 3rd Hussar Division, one half-company each.

————— 29, —— —— — — hospital of the 5th Infantry Corps.
————— 30, —— —— — — hospitals of the 15th and 12th Infantry Divisions, one half-company each.
————— 31, —— —— — — hospital of the 2nd Dragoon Division.
————— 32, —— —— — — hospital of the 6th Infantry Corps.
————— 33, —— —— — — hospitals of the 8th and 9th Infantry Divisions, one half-company each.
————— 34, formerly 33 — — hospital of the 3rd Dragoon Division.
————— 35, newly formed — — hospital of the Grenadier Corps.
————— 36, formerly 37 — — 3rd Grenadier Division and the Grenadier Corps, one half-company each.
————— 37, — 32 hospitals of the 2nd Reserve Cavalry Corps and 2nd Cuirassier Division, one half-company each.
————— 38, newly formed — hospitals of the 3rd Reserve Cavalry Corps and 3rd Lancer Division, one half-comp.each.
————— 39, formerly 45 — — hospital of the 4th Reserve Cavalry Corps.
————— 40, newly formed — — hospital of the 7th Infantry Corps.
————— 41, —— —— — — hospitals of the 18th and 22nd Infantry Divisions, one half-company each.
————— 42, —— —— — — hospital of the 8th Infantry Corps.
————— 43, —— —— — — hospitals of the 13th and 16th Infantry Divisions, one half-company each.
————— 44, —— ——— — St.-Petersburg Army Hospital [*Sukhoputnyi gospital*].
————— 45, —— ——— — ditto.
————— 46, —— ——— — ditto.
————— 47, —— ——— — ditto.
————— 48, —— —— — — St.-Petersburg Artillery Hospital.
————— 49, —— ——— — ditto.
————— 50, formerly 9 — — Oranienbaum Military Hospital.
————— 51, newly formed — — Reval Military Hospital.
————— 52, —— —— — — Narva, Novgorod, and Porkhov Military Hospitals, one-third company each.
————— 53, —— —— — — Moscow Military Hospital, one and two-thirds company,and at the Archangel Military Hospital, one-third company.
————— 54, —— —— — — ditto.
————— 55, —— —— — — Kazan and Omsk Military Hospitals, one half-company each.
————— 56, —— —— — — Kherson, Simferopol, and Phanagoria Military Hospitals, one-third company each.
————— 57, formerly 18 — — Viborg Military Hospital.
————— 58, newly formed — Abo [*Abovskii*] Military Hospital and the Separate Lithuania Corps, one half-comp. each.
————— 59, ——— Military Hospitals: Fredrikshamn, Helsingfors, and Aland, one-third company each.
————— 60, formerly 25 — — Headquarters of the 1st Army.
————— 61, ——— 29 — — ditto.
————— 62, ——— 24 — — 1st Infantry Corps.
————— 63, ——— 27 — — 2nd Infantry Corps.
————— 64, ——— 36 — — 3rd Infantry Corps.
————— 65, ——— 31 — — 4th Infantry Corps.
————— 66, ——— 34 — — 5th Infantry Corps.
————— 67, ——— 42 — — 6th Infantry Corps.
————— 68, ——— 38 — — Headquarters of the 2nd Army.
————— 69, ——— 39 — — ditto.
————— 70, ——— 43 — — 7th Infantry Corps.
————— 71, ——— 44 — — 8th Infantry Corps.

The last twelve companies, beginning with №60, were titled *Reserve [Rezervnaya]*, and all the previous ones indicated above (in the entry for 18 September, 1811) as №№1, 2, 3, 4, 8, 10, 11, and 12, were included in a special class under the title of *Guards Invalid Companies [Gvardeiskiya Invalidnyya roty]*, and therefore further information about them follows below, under Guards forces (330).

21 July 1816– For the Izhevsk Arms Factory, in addition to Mobile Invalid Company №14 already there, an additional Mobile Invalid Company №74was formed (331).

4 September 1816– In Irkutsk Province, for the Aleksandrovsk, Ilginsk, and Nikolaevsk distilleries [*vinokurennye zavody*] and the Irkutsk Salt Works [*solyanyi zavod*], there were established an Invalid half-company each, which together made up Mobile Invalid Companies №№75 and 76 (332).

29 October 1816– For the Tula Arms Factory, in addition to Mobile Invalid Company №11 already there, an additional Mobile Invalid Company №77 was formed (333).

In 1817– Mobile Invalid Company №78 was formed for the newly established hospitals of the Separate Georgia Corps, in Imeretia and at Yelisavetpol, one half-company for each (334).

22 June 1817– One half of Mobile Invalid Company №79 was established, designated for the Archangel Hospital (335).

28 December 1817– One half of Mobile Invalid Company №80 was established for the Warsaw Guards Hospital (336).

21 January 1818– The other half of Mobile Invalid Company №79 was established, designated for assignment at the Orenburg Corps Hospital (337).

8 August 1818– Mobile Invalid Company №81 was established to help Mobile Invalid Companies №№75 and 76 stationed at the factories of Irkutsk Province (338).

21 November 1818– Mobile Invalid Company №82 was established at St.-Petersburg Fortress (339).

19 February 1819– Mobile Invalid Company №83 was established at Schlüsselburg Fortress (340).

3 March 1819– Mobile Invalid Companies which were not at Army hospitals were ordered to receive new numbers:

№ 1 Company No. 1   With the 2nd Cadet Corps.

— 2 ——— — 2   Ditto.

— 3 ——— — 3   Ditto.

— 4 ——— — 82   At the St.-Petersburg Fortress and Alekseevsk Ravelin.

— 5 ——— — 4   — — Provisions Department [*Proviantskii Departament*].

— 6 ——— — 5   — — Aleksandrovsk Manufactory.

— 7 ——— — 6   Ditto.

— 8 ——— — 7   Ditto.

— 9 ——— — 8   Ditto.

— 10 ——— — 9   — — Sestroretsk Arms Factory.

— 11 ——— — 16   In Narva.

— 12 ——— — 83   At the Schlüsselburg Fortress.

— 13 ——— — 10   In Moscow, for Palace buildings.

— 14 ——— — 12   At the Pavlovsk State Cloth Factory.

— 15 ——— — 11   — — Tula Arms Factory.

— 16 ——— — 77   Ditto.

— 17 ——— — 13   — — Yekaterinoslavl State Cloth Factory.

— 18 ——— — 68   In Odessa, for trade quarantines.

— 19 ——— — 69   Ditto.

— 20 ——— — 14   At the Izhevsk Arms Factory.

— 21 ——— — 74   Ditto.

— 22 ——— — 75   In Irkutsk Province, at the distilleries: Aleksandrovsk, Nikolaevsk, and Ilginsk, and at the Irkutsk Salt Works .

— 23 ——— — 76   Ditto.

— 24 ——— — 81   Ditto (341).

2 December 1819– An additional *Mobile Invalid Company №17* was established to help Mobile Invalid Companies №№15 and 16 at the Tula Arms Factory. The previous company with this number, at the Yekaterinoslavl Cloth Factory, received №18, and the former company 18 at the Odessa trade quarantines was disbanded (342). Afterwards, by the year 1826, the distribution of all Mobile Invalid companies were as follows:

Company № 1   With the 2nd Cadet Corps, assigned to the St.-Petersburg Internal Garrison Battalion.

——— — 2   Ditto.

——— — 3   Ditto.

——— — 4   At the St.-Petersburg Fortress and Alekseevsk Ravelin, assigned to the same battalion.

——— — 5   With the Provisions Department, assigned to the same battalion.

——— — 6   At the Aleksandrovsk Manufactory, assigned to the same battalion.

——— — 7   Ditto.

——— — 8   Ditto.

——— — 9   Ditto.

———— — 10 At the Sestroretsk Arms Factory, assigned to the same battalion.

———— — 11 In Narva, to provide guard mounts, assigned to the same battalion.

———— — 12 At the Schlüsselburg Fortress, to provide guard mounts, assigned to the same battalion.

———— — 13 In Moscow, for Palace buildings, assigned to the Moscow Internal Garrison Battalion.

———— — 14 At the Pavlovsk State Cloth Factory, assigned to the same battalion.

———— — 15 At the Tula Arms Factory, assigned to the Internal Garrison battalion there.

———— — 16 Ditto.

———— — 17 Ditto.

———— — 19 At the Izhevsk Arms Factory.

———— — 20 Ditto.

———— — 21 In Irkutsk Province, at the Aleksandrovsk, Nikolaevsk, and Ilginsk distilleries, and the Irkutsk Salt Works.

———— — 22 Ditto.

———— — 23 Ditto.

———— — 24 At the St.-Petersburg Army Hospital.

———— — 25 Ditto.

———— — 26 Ditto.

———— — 27 The first half was at the same Army Hospital, and the second was at the Narva Hospital.

———— — 28 At the St.-Petersburg Artillery Hospital.

———— — 29 Two-thirds were at the same hospital, and one-third was for orderlies [*prislugi*] in the Court Hospital [*Pridvornyi gospital*] and other temporary detachments.

———— — 30 At the Oranienbaum Hospital.

———— — 31 — — Dünaburg ————

———— — 32 — — Riga ————

———— — 33 Two-thirds at the Riga Hospital and one-third at the Pernau Hospital.

———— — 34 At the Reval and Smolensk hospitals, one half-company each.

———— — 35 Two-thirds at the Kiev Hospital and one-third at the Dmitrovsk Hospital.

———— — 36 Ditto.

———— — 37 At the Moscow Hospital.

———— — 38 Ditto.

———— — 39 At the Moscow and Archangel hospitals, one half-company each.

———— — 40 — — Bobruisk Hospital.

———— — 41 — — Tiraspol Hospital.

———— — 42 — — Kamenets-Podolskii and Mogilev hospitals, one half-company each.

———— — 43 — — Tulchin and Simferopol hospitals, one half-company each.

———— — 44 — — Tiflis Hospital.

———— — 45 — — Kutais and Yelisavetpol hospitals, one half-company each.

———— — 46 — — Georgievsk Hospital.

———— — 47 — — Stavropol, Mozdok, and Vladikavkaz hospitals, one-third company each.

———— — 48 — — Helsingfors and Fredrikshamn hospitals, one half-company each.

———— — 49 — — Viborg, Aland, and Abo hospitals, one-third company each.

———— — 50 — — Warsaw Hospital, a half-company.

———— — 51 — — Grodno and Dubno [*Dubenskii*] hospitals, one half-company each.

———— — 52 — — Orenburg and Omsk hospitals, one half-company each.

———— — 53 — — Perm and Kazan hospitals, one half-company each.

———— — 54 With the Headquarters of the 1st Army.

———— — 55 Ditto.

———— — 56 With the 1st Corps.

———— — 57 —— — 2nd ——

———— — 58 —— — 3rd ——

———— — 59 —— — 4th —— and at the Bobruisk Hospital, one half-company each.

———— — 60 —— — 5th ——

———— — 61 —— — Grenadier Corps, three-fourths company, and at the Bryansk Lazaret, one-fourth.

——— — 62 —— — Headquarters of the 2nd Army.
——— — 63 —— — 6th Corps.
——— — 64 —— — 7th ——
——— — 65 At the Kherson Hospital [343].

b.) Serving and Non-serving Invalid Commands.

27 March 1811– With the general reorganization of invalids and their classification into Mobile, Serving, and Non-serving, from the remnants left in the various towns and fortresses of the Garrison regiments and battalions that were disbanded in this year, as well as from the personnel of the disbanded state district commands [*shtatnyya uezdnyya komandy*], there were established in the provinces [*gubernii*, or "governments"] the following *district Invalid commands* [*uezdnyya Invalidnyya komandy*]:

In *St.-Petersburg Province*: *Kronshtadtskaya* [Kronstadt], *Gdovskaya*, *Tsarskoselskaya* [Tsarskoe-Selo], *Yamburgskaya*, *Shlisselburgskaya* [Schlüsselburg], *Novoladozhskaya* [Novaya-Ladoga], and *Lugskaya* [Luga].

— *Livonia Province*: *Vendenskaya [Wenden], Derptskaya [Dorpat], Pernovskaya [Pernau],* and *Arensburgskaya.*

— *Estonia Province*: *Vezenbergskaya* [Wesenberg], *Veisenshteinskaya* [Weissenstein], *Gapsalskaya* [Hapsal], and *Baltiiskago Porta* [Baltic Port].

— *Finland Province*: *Fridrikhsgamskaya* [Fredrikshamn], *Vilmanstrandskaya* [Villmanstrand], *Neishlotskaya* [Nyslott], *Keksgolmskaya* [Kexholm], and *Serdobolskaya.*

— *Courland Province*: *Libavskaya* [Libau],*Gazenpotskaya* [Hasenpoth], *Vindavskaya* [Windau], *Goldingenskaya*, *Tukkumskaya*[Tuckum], and *Yakobshtadtskaya* [Jakobstadt].

— *Bialystok Region*: *Belskaya*[Bielsk], *Sokolskaya* [Sokoly], and *Dragochinskaya* [Drohiczyn].

— *Yekaterinoslavl Province*: *Novomoskovskaya*, *Pavlogradskaya*, *Bakhmutskaya*, *Slavyanoserbskaya*, *Rostovskaya*, *Aleksandrovskaya*, and *Verkhnedneprovskaya* [Verkhne-Dneprovsk].

— *Grodno Province*: *Volkoviskaya*, *Brest-Litovskaya*, *Pruzhanskaya* [Pruzhany], *Kobrinskaya*, *Lidskaya* [Lida], *Novogrudskaya* [Novogrudok], and *Slonimskaya.*

— *Caucasus Region [Kavkazskaya oblast]*: *Stavropolskaya*, *Aleksandrovskaya*, *Mozdokskaya*, and *Kizlyarskaya.*

— *Olonets Province*: *Olonetskaya*, *Ladeinopolskaya* [Lodeinoe-Pole], *Vytegorskaya* [Vytegra], *Pudozhskaya*, *Kargopolskaya*, and *Povenetskaya.*

— *Pskov Province*: *Porkhovskaya*,*Ostrovskaya*, *Opochetskaya* [Opochka], *Novorzhevskaya*, *Velikolutskaya* [Velikie-Luki], *Kholmovskaya* [Khlom], and *Toropetskaya.*

— *Saratov Province*: *Tsaritsynskaya*,*Kamyshinskaya*, *Balashevskaya* [Balashov], *Atkarskaya*, *Petrovskaya*, *Kuznetskaya*, *Velskaya* [Volsk], *Khvalynskaya*, and *Serdobskaya.*

— *Penza Province*: *Syzranskaya*, *Insarskaya*, *Krasnoslobodskaya*, *Narovchatskaya*, *Kerenskaya*, *Chembarskaya*, *Nizhnelomovskaya* [Nizhnii-Lovov], *Mokshanskaya*, and *Gorodishchenskaya* [Gorodishche].

— *Nizhnii-Novgorod Province*: *Arzamasskaya*, *Ardatovskaya*, *Balakhninskaya* [Balakhna], *Vasilskaya* [Vasil-Sursk], *Gorbatovskaya*, *Knyagininskaya*, *Lukoyanovskaya*, *Makarevskaya*, *Semenovskaya*, and *Sergachskaya.*

— *Kaluga Province*: *Tarusskaya* [Tarusa], *Maloyaroslavetskaya* , *Borovskaya*, *Medynskaya*, *Meshchovskaya*, *Masalskaya* [Mosalsk], *Zhizdrinskaya* [Zhizdra], *Kozelskaya*, *Peremyshlskaya*, and *Likhvinskaya.*

— *Tver Province*: *Novotorzhskaya*[Torzhok], *Vyshnevolotskaya* [Vyshnii-Volochek], *Staritskaya* [Staritsa], *Zubtsovskaya*, *Rzhevskaya*, *Ostashkovskaya*, *Kashinskaya*,*Kalyazinskaya*, *Vesegonskaya*, *Karchevskaya* [Korcheva], and *Bezhetskaya.*

— *Smolensk Province*: *Krasnenskaya*[Krasnyi], *Dukhovshchinskaya* [Dukhovshchina], *Porechskaya* [Poreche], *Dorogobuzhskaya*, *Yelninskaya* [Yelna], *Roslavlskaya*, *Belskaya* [Beloi, or Belyi], *Vyazemskaya* [Vyazma], *Yukhnovskaya*, *Gzhatskaya*, and *Sychevskaya* [Sychevka].

— *Ryazan Province*: *Zaraiskaya*, *Pronskaya*, *Skopinskaya* , *Spasskaya*, *Kasimovskaya*, *Sapozhkovskaya* [Sapozhok], *Ryazhskaya*, *Ranenburgskaya*, *Dankovskaya*, *Mikhailovskaya*, and *Yegorevskaya.*

— *Tambov Province*: *Kozlovskaya*,*Morshanskaya*, *Shatskaya* , *Yelatomskaya* [Yelatma], *Temnikovskaya*, *Spasskaya*, *Kirsanovskaya*, *Borisoglebskaya*, *Usmanskaya*, *Lebedyanskaya*, and *Lipetskaya.*

— *Tula Province*: *Aleksinskaya*, *Kashirskaya* [Kashira], *Venevskaya*, *Bogoroditskaya*, *Yepifanskaya*, *Yefremovskaya*,*Novosilskaya*, *Chernskaya*, *Krapivinskaya* [Krapivna], *Odoevskaya* [Odoevo], and *Belevskaya.*

— *Vladimir Province*: *Aleksandrovskaya*, *Vyaznikovskaya* [Vyazniki], *Gorokhovetskaya*, *Kovrovskaya*,*Melenkovskaya* [Melenki], *Muromskaya*,*Pereslavlskaya*,*Pokrovskaya*,*Sudogodskaya* [Sudogda],*Suzdalskaya*,*Shuiskaya* [Shuya],and *Yurevskaya.*

— *Voronezh Province*: *Zadonskaya*,*Zemlyanskaya*, *Nizhnedevitskaya*, *Korotoyakskaya*,*Ostrogozhskaya*, *Biryuchskaya*,*Valuiskaya*

[Valuiki],*Bogucharskaya,Pavlovskaya,Novokhoperskaya,Bobrovskaya,*and *Starobelskaya.*

— *Kursk Province:* Novooskolskaya[Novyi-Oskol],*Starooskolskaya* [Staryi-Oskol], *Timskaya, Shchigrovskaya* [Shchigry],*Khotmyzhskaya, Rylskaya,Lgovskaya,Sudzhenskaya* [Sudzha],*Fatezhskaya,Dmitrievskaya,Oboyanskaya,Belgorodskaya,Korochanskaya,*and *Putivlskaya.*

— *Novgorod Province:* Starorussskaya[Staraya-Russa],*Krestetskaya* [Kresttsy], *Valdaiskaya, Borovitskaya* [Borovichi], *Ustyuzhskaya* [Ustyuzhna], *Cherepovetsskaya,Kirilovskaya,Belozerskaya,*and *Tikhvinskaya.*

— *Vologda Province:* Gryazovetskaya,Kadnikovskaya, *Totemskaya* [Totma], *Velikoustyugskaya* [Velikii-Ustyug], *Volskaya* [Velsk], *Nikolskaya, Yarenskaya, Solvychegodskaya,*and *Ustsysolskaya* [Ust-Sysolsk].

— *Yaroslavl Province:* Rostovskaya, Uglichskaya, Rybinskaya, Romanov-Borisoglebskaya, Danilovskaya, Mologskaya [Mologa],*Lyubimskaya, Poshekhonskaya,* and *Myshkinskaya.*

— *Slobodsko-Ukraine Province:* Volkovskaya[Valki], Bogodukhovskaya, Akhtyrskaya [Akhtyrka], *Lebedyanskaya,Sumskaya* [Sumy], *Zmievskaya,Izyumskaya,Kupyanskaya,*and *Volchanskaya.*

— *Minsk Province:* Vilenskaya[sic, should be Vileiskaya],*Disnenskaya* [Disna], *Borisovskaya, Igumenskaya,Bobruiskaya, Rechitskaya* [Rechitsa],*Mozyrskaya,Slutskaya,*and *Pinskaya.*

— *Vilna Province:* Trokskaya[Troki],*Kovnenskaya* [Kovno], *Rossienskaya* [Rossieny], *Telshevskaya* [Telshi],*Shavelskaya* [Shavli], *Upitskaya,Vilkomirskaya,Vidzynskaya* [Vidzy],*Oshmyanskaya* [Oshmyany], and *Zavileiskaya.*

—*Kostroma Province:* Nerekhotskaya[Nerekhta],*Kineshemskaya*[Kineshma],*Yurevets-Povolskaya,Soligalichskaya,Chukhlomskaya* [Chukhloma], *Varnavinskaya,Vetlugskaya* [Vetluga],*Galichskaya,Buevskaya* [Bui], *Makarevskaya,*and *Kologrivskaya.*

— *Orel Province:* Mtsenskaya,Bolkhovskaya, Karachevskaya, Bryanskaya,Trubchevskaya, Sevskaya,Dmitrovskaya,Kromskaya [Kromy],*Maloarkhangelskaya,Livenskaya* [Livny],and *Yeletskaya.*

— *Perm Province:* Okhanskaya, Osinskaya [Osa], Kungurskaya, Krasnoufimskaya, Yekaterinburgskaya, Shadrinskaya, Kamyshlovskaya, Irbitskaya, Verkhoturevskaya, Solikamskaya, < i>and *Cherdynskaya.*

— *Kiev Province:* Radomyslskaya,Makhnovskaya [Makhnovka], *Lipovetskaya, Umanskaya,Zvenigorodskovskaya* [Zvenigorodka], *Cherkasskaya* [Cherkassy],*Chigirinskaya,Boguslavlskaya,Tarashchinskaya* [Tarashcha],*Skvirskaya* [Skvira],and *Vasilkovskaya.*

— *Vitebsk Province:* Surazhskaya, Velizhskaya, Gorodetskaya [Gorodok], Nevelskaya, Lepelskaya, Polotskaya, Sebezhskaya, *Lyutsinskaya, Rezhitskaya* [Rezhitsa], *Dinaburgskaya* [Dünaburg],and *Drizenskaya* [Drissa].

— *Mogilev Province:* Mstislavskaya[Mstislavl],*Starobykhovskaya* [Staryi-Bykhov], *Kopysskaya* [Kopys], *Babinovichskaya,Cherikovskaya, Klimovetskaya,Senninskaya* [Senno],*Belitskaya,Rogachevskaya, Orshanskaya* [Orsha],and *Chausskaya* [Chausy].

— *Volhynia Province:* Novgrad-Volynskaya, Zaslavlskaya, Ostrogskaya, Rovenskaya [Rovno], Ovruchskaya, Lutskaya, Vladimirskaya, Kovelskaya, Starokonstantinovskaya, Dubenskaya [Dubno], and *Kremenetskaya.*

— *Chernigov Province:* Gorodnyanskaya[Gorodnya],*Novozybkovskaya, Surazhskaya, Mglinskaya,Starodubskaya, Novgorod-Severskaya, Glukhovskaya, Krolevetskaya, Sosnitskaya* [Sosnitsa], *Konotopskaya, Borznenskaya* [Borzna], *Nezhinskaya, Kozeletskaya,*and *Osterskaya.*

— *Poltava Province:* Romenskaya[Romny],*Lubenskaya* [Lubny], *Kremenchugskaya, Zolotonoshskaya* [Zolotonoshcha], *Kobylyakskaya* [Kobelyaki], *Pereyaslavskaya* [Pereyaslavl],*Gadyachskaya,Zenkovskaya,Konstantinogradskaya, Prilukskaya* [Priluki],*Piryatinskaya,Mirgorodskaya,Lokhvitskaya* [Lokhvitsa],and *Khorolskaya.*

— *Podolia Province:* Proskurovskaya,Letichevskaya, Litinskaya, Vinnitskaya [Vinnitsa], Bratslavskaya, Gaisinskaya, Olgopolskaya, Baltskaya [Balta], Yampolskaya, Mogilevskaya (na Dnestre) [Mogilev (on the Dniester)], and *Utitskaya* [sic, should be *Ushitskaya*].

— *Moscow Province:* Bogorodskaya,Bronnitskaya [Bronnitsy], Vereiskaya [Vereya], Volokolamskaya, Dmitrovskaya, Kolomenskaya [Kolomna], Zvenigorodskaya, Klinskaya, Mozhaiskaya, Podolskaya, Ruzskaya [Ruzha], and *Serpukhovskaya.*

—*Astrakhan Province:* Krasnoyarskaya [Krasnyi-Yar], Chernoyarskaya [Chernyi-Yar], and *Yenotaevskaya.*

— *Kherson Province:* Aleksandriiskaya [Aleksandriya], Yelisavetgradskaya, Olviopolskaya, and *Tiraspolskaya.*

— *Taurica Province:* Yevpatoriiskaya[Yevpatoria], Perekopskaya, Aleshkovskaya [Aleshki], Orekhovskaya, and *Theodosiiskaya* .

— *Archangel Province:* Kholmogorskaya [Kholmogory], Shenkurskaya, Pinegskaya [Pinega], Kemskaya, Mezenskaya, Onegskaya [Onega], and *Kolskaya* [Kola].

— *Vyatka Province:* Slobodskaya[Slobodskoi],*Glazovskaya, Sarapulskaya, Yelabugskaya* [Yelabuga], *Urzhumskaya, Nolinskaya, Yaranskaya, Kotelnitskaya* [Kotelnich], and *Orlovskaya.*

— *Simbirsk Province:* Stavropolskaya,Korsunskaya, Samarskaya [Samara], Buinskaya, Sengileevskaya [Sengilei], Syzranskaya, Ardatovskaya, Alatyrskaya, and *Kurmyzhskaya* [Kurmysh].

— *Kazan Province: Sviyazhskaya, Tsivilskaya, Cheboksarskaya* [Cheboksary], *Kozmodemyanskaya, Yadrinskaya, Tsarevokokshaiskaya, Laishevskaya, Chistopolskaya, Mamadyshskaya, Tetyushskaya* [Tetyushi], and *Spasskaya.*

— *Orenburg Province: Menzelinskaya, Birskaya, Bugulminskaya* [Bugulma], *Belebeevskaya* [Belebei], *Buguruslanskaya, Buzulukskaya, Orenburgskaya, Sterlitamakskaya, Verkhneuralskaya* [Verkhne-Uralsk], *Troitskaya,* and *Chelyabinskaya.*

In each province [*guberniya*] these commands were assigned to the Garrison battalions and half-battalions stationed in the provincial cities (344).

21 December 1811 – The District Invalid commands of Moscow, Astrakhan, Kazan, and Archangel provinces came under the control of the Garrison regiments there (345).

31 December 1815 – The Tsarskoe-Selo District Invalid Command was disbanded (346).

12 July 1816 – Serving District Invalid commands were established: the *Signakhskaya, Telavskaya, Ananurskaya,* and *Goriiskaya [Gori]*, which came under the control of the Tiflis Internal Garrison Battalion (347).

4 September 1816 – With the establishment of the Internal Guard in the Siberian provinces, Serving Invalid commands were formed: the *Tyumenskaya, Yalutorovskaya, Ishimskaya, Omskaya, Turinskaya, Kurganskaya,* and *Tarskaya [Tara]*, all assigned to the Tobolsk Garrison battalion; the *Yeniseiskaya, Kainskaya, Biiskaya, Kuznetskaya, Narymskaya,* and *Krasnoyarskaya,* all assigned to the Tomsk Garrison Battalion; and the *Kirenskaya, Nerchinskaya, Yakutskaya, Verkhneudinskaya,* and *Nizhneudinskaya,* all assigned to the Irkutsk Garrison Regiment. Along with this, Non-serving Invalid commands were established: the *Tomskaya, Yalutorovskaya, Kurganskaya, Ishimskaya, Tarskaya [Tara], Omskaya, Krasnoyarskaya, Biiskaya, Kuznetskaya, and Kainskaya* (348).

25 October 1816 – Commands of Serving and Non-serving invalids were established in all provincial capitals [*gubernskie goroda*] and regional seats [*oblastnye goroda*]: St. Petersburg, Riga, Reval, Viborg, Kuopio, Mitau, Bialystok, Yekaterinoslavl, Grodno, Georgievsk, Petrozavodsk, Pskov, Saratov, Penza, Nizhnii-Novgorod, Kaluga, Tver, Smolensk, Ryazan, Tambov, Tula, Vladimir, Voronezh, Kursk, Novgorod, Vologda, Yaroslavl, Kharkov, Minsk, Vilna, Kostroma, Orel, Perm, Kiev, Vitebsk, Mogilev, Zhitomir, Chernigov, Poltava, Kamenets-Podolskii, Moscow, Astrakhan, Kherson, Simferopol, Archangel, Vyatka, Simbirsk, Kazan, Orenburg, Tiflis, Tobolsk, Tomsk, Irkutsk, and Kishinev (349).

15 November 1816 – It was ordered to have commands of Serving and Non-serving invalids with the Settled regiments, transferring to this status those lower ranks who had become unfit for the continuation of field and garrison service (350).

8 March 1817 – The *Malmyzhskaya Sluzhashchaya Invalidnaya komanda [Malmyzh Serving Invalid Command]* was established, subordinate to the Vyatka Internal Garrison Battalion (351).

5 May 1817 – Of the district Invalid commands administered by the Viborg Internal Garrison Battalion, the *Nyslott* was transferred to the control of the Kuopio Internal Garrison Battalion (352).

29 May 1817 – District commands of Serving invalids were established: the *Izmailskaya, Khotinskaya, Akkermanskaya, Kiliiskaya [Kiliya],* and *Benderskaya [Bendery]*, which came under the control of the Kishinev Internal Garrison Battalion (353).

15 June 1819 – The *Konstantinogorskaya Invalidnaya komanda* was established for the Caucasus mineral waters, subordinate to the Georgievsk Internal Garrison Battalion (354).

19 October 1819 – The Nyslott and, established on 25 October, 1816, Kuopio District Invalid Commands came under the control of the Viborg Garrison Regiment (355).

18 August 1821 – The *Odesskaya Invalidnaya komanda [Odessa Invalid Command]* was established, assigned to the Kherson Internal Garrison Battalion (356).

10 September 1821 – With the disestablishment [*uprazdnenie*] of the town of Ananur, the district Invalid command there was transferred to the town of Dushet and named the *Dushetskaya* (357).

15 May 1822 – The Kiliya District Invalid Command was transferred to the town of Belitsy and named the *Belitskaya* (358).

5 January 1823 – There were established: the *Achinskaya, Minusinskaya, and Kanskaya* commands of Serving and Non-serving invalids, coming under the control of the Krasnoyarsk Garrison Battalion, and to this battalion were also assigned the Krasnoyarsk and Yeniseisk District Invalid Commands, which had been under the Tomsk Garrison Battalion (359).

16 Januray 1823 – With the disestablishment of the town of Aleksandrovsk, the Aleksandrovsk District Invalid Command, located there and administered by the Georgievsk Internal Garrison Battalion, was disbanded (360).

19 April 1823 – All Non-serving invalids were completely released from service and that status abolished (361).

14 August 1823 – There were established: the *Tyukalinskaya* and *Charymskaya Invalidnyya komandy*, the first assigned to the Tobolsk Garrison Battalion and the second to the Tomsk (362).

5 April 1824 – In the newly established town of Kolyvan, it was ordered to establish the *Kolyvanskaya uezdnaya Invalidnaya komanda*, subordinating it to the Tomsk Garrison Battalion (363).

14 July 1824 – The *Bakchisaraiskaya Invalidnaya komanda* was established, designated for maintaining guard details in the demoted [*zashtatnyi*] town of Bakchisarai and subordinated to the Taurica Internal Garrison Battalion (364).

7 December 1824– The Staraya-Russa District Invalid Command was transferred to the newly established town of Demyansk in Novgorod Province and named the *Demyanskaya* (365).

18 February 1825– With the transfer of the town of Starobelsk from Voronezh Province to Slobodsko-Ukraine Province, the Starobelsk District Invalid Command came under the control of the Kharkov Internal Garrison Battalion (366).

By 1826– Administered by Garrison regiments and battalions, *Invalid commands* were as follows:

In the Livonia, Estonia, Courland, Yekaterinoslavl, Grodno, Olonets, Pskov, Saratov, Penza, Nizhnii-Novgorod, Kaluga, Tver, Smolensk, Ryazan, Tambov, Tula, Vladimir, Kursk, Vologda, Yaroslavl, Minsk, Vilna, Kostroma, Orel, Perm, Kiev, Vitebsk, Mogilev, Chernigov, Poltava, Podolia, Moscow, Astrakhan, Archangel, Simbirsk, Kazan, and Orenburg provinces, in the Bialystok Region, and in Finland, all commands were as established in 1811 for district towns and in 1816 for provincial cities.

In St.-Petersburg Province: all the commands that were established in 1811 and 1816 except the Tsarskoe-Selo, which was disbanded in 1815.

— *Voronezh Province:* all the commands that were established in 1811 and 1816 except the Starobelsk, which in 1825 was transferred to Slobodsko-Ukraine Province.

— *Slobodsko-Ukraine Province:* all the commands that were established in 1811 and 1816, plus the Starobelsk.

— *Novgorod Province:* all the commands that were established in 1811 and 1816, with only the Staraya-Russa being transferred to Demyansk.

— *Kherson Province:* all the commands that were established in 1811 and 1816, plus the Odessa, formed in 1821.

— *Taurica Province:* all the commands that were established in 1811 and 1816, plus the Bakchisarai, formed in 1824.

— *Vyatka Province:* all the commands that were established in 1811 and 1816, plus the Malmyzh, formed in 1817.

— *Caucasus Region:* all the commands that were established in 1811 and 1816 except the Aleksandrovsk, disbanded in 1823, and with the addition of the Konstantinogorsk, in existence from 1819.

— *Georgia:* all the commands established in 1816.

— *Tobolsk Province:* all the commands that were established in 1816, plus the Tyukalinsk, formed in 1823.

— *Tomsk Province:* all the commands that were established in 1816, except the Yeniseisk and Krasnoyarsk which in 1823 were transferred to Yeniseisk Province, and plus the Charymsk and Kolyvan, which were formed in 1823 and 1824.

— *Yeniseisk Province:* the commands thatwere transferred from Tomsk Province and those newly established in 1823: the Yeniseisk, Krasnoyarsk, Achinsk, Minusinsk, and Kansk.

— *Bessarabia Province:* all the commands that were established in 1817, with only the transfer of the Kiliya to Belitsy [367].

c.) Étape Invalid Commands.

9 May 1817– With the establishment of étapes for conveying prisoners along the route from St. Petersburg to Moscow, there were formed, under the administration of the Internal Guard battalions, *Étape Invalid commands [Etapnyya Invalidnyya komandy]:*

Novgorod Battalion: – the *Ushakovskaya,Chudovskaya,Bronnitskaya,*and *Kuzhenkinskaya.*

Moscow Battalion: – the *Voskresenskaya* and *Chashnikovskaya* [368].

4 July 1817– The Chudovo Étape Command was transferred to Syabrintsa and named the *Syabrinskaya* (369).

21 August 1817– With the establishment of étapes for conveying prisoners along the route from Moscow past Kazan and Perm and through Tobolsk Province, there were formed, under the administration of the regiments and battalions of the Internal Guard, *Étape commands:*

Nizhnii-Novgorod Battalion: – the *Slobodskaya* and *Ostashikhinskaya.*

Kazan Regiment: – the *Vilovatoovragskaya, Akazevoizmenskaya, Arkhangelskaya,* and *Koreduvanskaya.*

Vyatka Battalion: – the *Bolshekillezskaya, Syumsa-Mozhginskaya, Chenyabinskaya, Zyattsynskaya,* and *Debesskaya.*

Perm Regiment: – the *Sosnovskaya, Yanychinskaya, Zlatoustovskaya, Biserskaya, Grabovskaya, Byleiskaya,*and *Pylaevskaya* [370].

10 January 1818– With the establishment of étapes for conveying prisoners along the route from St. Petersburg to Archangel and Riga, there were formed, under the administration of the regiments and battalions of the Internal Guard, *Étape commands:*

St.-Petersburg Battalion: – the *Vystavskaya* and *Kaskovskaya.*

Petrozavodsk Battalion: – the *Gomarovichskaya, Burkovskaya, Arkhangelskaya,* and *Thedotovskaya.*

Novgorod Battalion: – the *Krechetovskaya.*

Archangel Regiment: – the *Tarasovskaya* and *Tegrinskaya.*

Riga Battalion: – the *Valkskaya* and *Nenalskaya.*

Reval Battalion: – the *Yeveskaya* [371].

5 February 1818– With the establishment of étapes for conveying prisoners along the route from Kiev through Vitebsk, Velikie-Luki, and Porkhov to St. Petersburg, there were formed, under the administration of the battalions of the Internal Guard, *Étape commands:*

    Minsk Battalion: – the *Loevskaya.*

    Pskov Battalion: – the *Porkhovinskaya* and *Sorokinskaya.*

    St.-Petersburg Battalion: – the *Theofilovskaya* and *Rozhestvenskaya* [372].

12 February 1818– With the establishment of étapes for conveying prisoners along the routes: 1) from Grodno through Vilna, Druya, and Pskov to Theofilovaya Pustynya; 2) from Brest-Litovsk through Minsk and Smolensk to Moscow; 3) from Grodno to the small town of Novyi-Sverzhen; and 4) from Kazan to Orenburg, there were formed, under the administration of the regiments and battalions of the Internal Guard, *Étape commands:*

    Grodno Battalion: – the *Kamenkovskaya,Bylitskaya,Ruzhanskaya,*and *Stolovichskaya.*

    Vilna Battalion: – the *Soleshnikovskaya* and *Bratslavskaya.*

    Minsk Battalion: – the *Novosverzhenskaya,Kaidanovskaya,*and *Smolevichskaya.*

    Vitebsk Battalion: – the *Rositskaya.*

    Mogilev Battalion: – the *Tolochinskaya.*

    Smolensk Battalion: – the *Pnevskaya.*

    Pskov Battalion: – the *Dubrovskaya.*

    Kazan Battalion: – the *Kuchu-Adamchatskaya* [373].

20 September 1818– Of the Étape commands of Vyatka Province, the Chenyabinsk was transferred to the settlement of Selty and renamed the *Seltynskaya* (374).

10 May 1819– With the establishment of étapes for conveying prisoners along the routes from Odessa to Kiev and from Brest-Litovsk to Dubno, there were formed, under the administration of the battalions of the Internal Guard, *Étape commands:*

    Kherson Battalion: – the *Dubossarskaya.*

    Zhitomir Battalion: – the *Ratninskaya* [375].

19 January 1820– With the establishment of étapes for conveying prisoners from St. Petersburg to Viborg and from Riga through Dünaburg, Vitebsk, and Orsha to the étape road established from Brest-Litovsk to Moscow, there were formed, under the administration of the battalions of the Internal Guard, *Étape commands:*

    Viborg Battalion: – the *Krasnoselskaya.*

    Riga Battalion: – the *Gross-Yungsferngofskaya.*

    Mitau Battalion: – the *Illyukstinskaya* [376].

1 April 1821– With the establishment of étapes for conveying prisoners from Moscow to the town of Aleksandrov in Vladimir Province, there were formed, under the administration of the Moscow Internal Garrison Battalion, *Étape commands: Sergievskaya* and *Burtsovskaya* (377).

1 June 1821– The *Kirgishanskaya Etapnaya komanda* was established in Perm Province, and the *Grabovskaya* and *Bileiskaya* were transferred to other settlements and, accordingly, received the names: for the first—*Bilimbeevskaya,* and for the second—*Beloyarskaya* (378).

19 February 1822– With the establishment of étapes for conveying prisoners from Kherson through Berislav to the towns of the Taurica peninsula, there were formed, under the administration of the battalions of the Internal Guard, *Étape commands:*

    Kherson Battalion: – the *Berislavskaya.*

    Taurica Battalion: – the *Bakchisaraiskaya* [379].

16 July 1822– With the establishment of étapes for conveying prisoners along the route from Kherson to Odessa, and also from Kherson through Yelisavetgrad and Aleksandriya to Kremenchug, there were formed, under the administration of the Kherson Internal Guard Battalion, *Étape commands: Nikolaevskaya* and *Vassiyat-skaya* (380).

22 July 1822– With the establishment of étapes for conveying exiles through the Siberian provinces, there were formed *Étape commands* subordinate to the garrisons there:

    Tobolsk Battalion – Étape commands of Tobolsk Province, from №1 to №19 inclusive.

    Tomsk Battalion – Étape commands of Tomsk Province, from №1 to №21, and of Yeniseisk Province, from №1 to №8 inclusive.

    Irkutsk Battalion – Étape commands of Irkutsk Province, from №1 to №13 inclusive [381].

10 October 1822– With the establishment of étapes for conveying prisoners along the route from Novaya-Ladoga through

Yaroslavl and Kostroma to Nizhnii-Novgorod, there was formed, under the administration of the Novgorod Internal Guard Battalion, the *Sominskaya Etapnaya komanda* (382).

17 October 1822– With the establishment of étapes for conveying prisoners along the route from the town of Ufa through Birsk and Krasnoufimsk to Siberia, there was formed, under the administration of the Ufa Internal Guard Battalion, the *Askinskaya Etapnaya komanda* (383).

2 December 1822– With the establishment of étapes for conveying prisoners along the route from Tambov through Chembary and Penza to Simbirsk, there were formed, under the administration of battalions of the Internal Guard, *Étape commands:*

Simbirsk Battalion: – the *Yurlovskaya.*

Penza Battalion: – the *Kamenskaya.*

Tambov Battalion: – the *Raskazovskaya* [384].

5 January 1823– With the establishment of the Krasnoyarsk Garrrison Battalion, *Étape commands of Yeniseisk Province, from №1 to №8* inclusive, were subordinated to this battalion (385).

1 December 1823– Of the Étape commands under the administration of the Archangel Garrison Regiment, the *Tegrinskaya* was transferred to the Siisk Tract [*pogost*] and named the *Siiskaya* (386).

12 January 1824– For improving the conveyance of prisoners from Simbirsk to Kazan, there was formed the *Burundukskaya Etapnaya komanda*, assigned to the Kazan Garrison Regiment (387).

27 February 1824– Étape commands in the Siberian provinces were directed to be named not by numbers, but in accordance with the places where the étapes were stationed:

In Tobolsk Province: Command №1, as the *Tugulymskaya.*

——— 2, — — *Perevalovskaya.*

——— 3, — — *Sozonovskaya.*

——— 4, — — *Yuzhakovskaya.*

——— 5, — — *Bachalinskaya.*

——— 6, — — *Kutarbinskaya.*

——— 7, — — *Staropogostskaya.*

——— 8, — — *Dresvyanskaya.*

——— 9, — — *Balakhleiskaya.*

——— 10, — — *Chistyakovskaya.*

——— 11, — — *Vikulovskaya.*

——— 12, — — *Achimovskaya.*

——— 13, — — *Verkhoaevskaya.*

——— 14, — — *Rybinskaya.*

——— 15, — — *Chauninskaya.*

——— 16, — — *Znamenskaya.*

——— 17, — — *Tarskaya.*

——— 18, — — *Meshkovskaya.*

——— 19, — — *Kopevskaya.*

In Tomsk Province: Command № 1, — — *Murashinskaya.*

——— 2, — — *Voznesenskaya.*

——— 3, — — *Turumovskaya.*

——— 4, — — *Antoshkinskaya.*

——— 5, — — *Osinovskaya.*

——— 6, — — *Ubinskaya.*

——— 7, — — *Kargatskaya.*

——— 8, — — *Itkulskaya.*

——— 9, — — *Ovchinnikovskaya.*

——— 10, — — *Tyryshkinskaya.*

——— 11, — — *Orskaya.*

——— 12, — — *Tatarinskaya.*

——— 13, — — *Bolotininskaya.*

——— 14, — — *Varyukhinskaya.*

——— 15, — — *Khaldeevskaya.*
——— 16, — — *Ishimskaya.*
——— 17, — — *Pochitanskaya.*
——— 18, — — *Podelnichnaya.*
——— 19, — — *Suslovskaya.*
——— 20, — — *Itatskaya.*
——— 21, — — *Krasnorechinskaya.*

In Yeniseisk Province: Command № 1, — — *Klyuchinskaya.*
——— 2, — — *Maloingatskaya.*
——— 3, — — *Kanskaya.*
——— 4, — — *Klyuchevskaya.*
——— 5, — —*Uyarskaya.*
——— 6, — — *Kuskunskaya.*
——— 7, — — *Malonemchugskaya.*
——— 8, — —*Kozulskaya.*

In Irkutsk Province: Command № 1, — — *Bilitkuiskaya.*
——— 2, — —*Polovinskaya.*
——— 3, — — *Kutulitskaya.*
——— 4, — — *Tyretskaya.*
——— 5, — — *Kimilteiskaya.*
——— 6, — — *Kuitunskaya.*
——— 7, — — *Sharagulskaya.*
——— 8, — — *Kurzanskaya.*
——— 9, — — *Khudoelanskaya.*
——— 10, — —*Ukovskaya.*
——— 11, — —*Algashetskaya.*
——— 12, — — *Razgonskaya.*
——— 13, — —*Biryusinskaya* [388].

3 May 1824– With the establishment of étapes for conveying prisoners along the route from Georgievsk past Stavropol to Rostov, through the Caucasus Region and the Land of the Don Cossacks, there were formed: the *Aleksandrovskaya,* *Medyzhinskaya,* and *Mechetinskaya Etapnyya komandy,* of which the first two came under the administration of Georgievsk, while the last was located in the Land of the Don Host [389].

10 May 1824– There were formed: the *Konstanskaya* and *Kazachinskaya Etapnyya komandy,* subordinate to the Krasnoyarsk Garrison Battalion [390].

28 January 1825– The Mechetinskaya Étape Command was disbanded [391].

17 July 1825– Of the Etape commands administered by the St.-Petersburg Internal Garrison Battalion, the *Rozhestvenskaya* was transferred to the village of Yashchery and named the *Yashcherskaya* [392]. After this, by 20 November of this year there were the following Étape commands administered by Garrison regiments and battalions:

With the Mitau Battalion — *Illyukstinskaya.*
— — — Riga ———*Balkskaya,* *Nenalskaya,* and *Gross-Yungferngofskaya.*
— — — Reval ——— *Yeveskaya.*
— — — Pskov ———*Porkhovinskaya,* *Sorokinskaya,* and *Dubrovskaya.*
— — — Smolensk ——— *Pnevskaya.*
— — — Vitebsk ———*Rositskaya.*
— — — Mogilev ———*Tolochinskaya.*
— — — Kherson ——— *Nikolaevaskaya,* *Vassiyatskaya,* *Dubosarskaya,* and *Berislavskaya.*
— — — Viborg Regiment — *Krasnoselskaya.*
— — — Archangel ———*Tarasovskaya* and *Siiskaya.*
— — — Petrozavodsk Battalion —*Gomarovichskaya,* *Burkovskaya,* *Arkhangelskaya,* and *Thedotovskaya.*
— — — St.-Petersburg ———*Vystavskaya,* *Kaskovskaya,* *Theofilovskaya,* and *Yashcherskaya.*
— — — Novgorod ———*Ushakovskaya,* *Syabrinskaya,* *Bronnitskaya,* *Kuzhenkinskaya,* and *Krechetovskaya.*
— — — Moscow ———*Chashnikovskaya,* *Voskresenskaya,* and *Sergievskaya.*

—— — Tambov ———— *Raskazovskaya.*

—— — Vyatka ————*Bolshe-Killezskaya, Syumsa-Mozhginskaya, Seltynskaya, Zyattsyn-skaya,* and *Debesskaya.*

—— — Perm ————*Sosnovskaya, Yanychinskaya, Zlatoustovskaya, Biserskaya, Bilimbeevskaya, Kirgishenskaya, Beloyarskaya,* and *Pylaevskaya.*

—— — Ufa ———*Askinskaya.*

—— — Nizhnii-Novgorod ——— *Slobodskaya* and *Astashikhinskaya* [sic, previously spelled *Ostashikinskaya*].

—— — Simbirsk ———*Yurlovskaya.*

—— — Penza ——— *Kamenskaya.*

—— — Kazan Regiment —— *Vilovatoovragskaya, Akazevoismenskaya, Arkhangelskaya, Koreduvanskaya, Kuchu-Adamchatskaya,* and *Burundukskaya.*

—— — Stavropol Battalion — *Aleksandrovskaya* and *Medvezhinskaya.*

—— — Vilna ——— *Soleshnikovskaya* and *Bratslavskaya.*

—— — Minsk ——— *Loevskaya, Novo-Sverzhenskaya, Kaidanovskaya,* and *Smolevichskaya.*

—— — Grodno ——— *Kamenkovskaya, Belitskaya, Ruzhanskaya,* and *Stolovichskaya.*

—— — Zhitomir ——— *Ratninskaya.*

—— — Tobolsk ——— *Tugulymskaya, Perevalovskaya, Sozonovskaya, Yuzhakovskaya, Bochalinskaya* [sic, previously spelled *Bachalinskaya*], *Kutarbinskaya, Staropogostskaya, Dresvyanskaya, Balakhleiskaya, Chistyakovskaya, Vikulovskaya, Achimovskaya, Verkhoaevskaya, Rybinskaya, Chauninskaya, Znamenskaya, Tarskaya, Meshkovskaya,* and *Kopevskaya.*

—— — Tomsk ——— *Murashinskaya, Voznesenskaya, Turumovskaya, Antoshkinskaya, Osinovskaya, Ubinskaya, Kargatskaya, Itkulskaya, Ovchinnikovskaya, Tyryshkinskaya, Orskaya, Tatarinskaya, Bolotinskaya, Varyukhinskaya, Khaldeevskaya, Ishimskaya, Pochitanskaya, Podelnichnaya, Suslovskaya, Itatskaya,* and *Krasnorechinskaya.*

—— — Krasnoyarsk ——— *Klyuchinskaya, Maloingatskaya, Kanskaya, Klyuchevskaya, Uyarskaya, Kuskunskaya, Malokemchugskaya, Kozulskaya, Konstanskaya,* and *Kazachinskaya.*

—— — Irkutsk Regiment — *Biliktuiskaya, Polovinskaya, Kutulitskaya, Tyretskaya, Kimiltei-skaya, Kuitunskaya, Sharagulskaya, Kurzanskaya, Khudoelanskaya, Ukovskaya, Algashetskaya, Razgonskaya,* and *Biryusinskaya* [393].

d.) Salt Invalid Commands.

5 August 1818– For maintaining guard details for Salt works [*Solyanye promysly*], there were formed *Serving Invalid commands* under the title *Salt commands:* the *Kamyshinskaya, Astrakhanskaya, Mozharskaya, Starorusskaya [Staraya-Russa], Dedyukhinskaya [Dedyukhino], Onegskaya [Onega],* and *Ledengskaya [Ledengskoe]* (394).

12 August 1818– These commands were assigned to regiments and battalions of the Internal Guard:

Kamyshinskaya — to the Saratov Battalion.
Astrakhanskaya —— — Astrakhan Regiment.
Mozharskaya —— —Georgievsk Battalion.
Starorusskaya —— —Novgorod———
Dedyukhinskaya —— — Perm ——
Onegskaya —— — Archangel Regiment.
Ledengskaya —— —Vologda Battalion [395].

23 April 1819– The *Crimea Salt Command* [*Krymskaya Solyanaya komanda*], which had existed at the Crimea Salt works since 1805 under the control of the Ministry of Finances, was assigned to the Taurica Internal Guard Battalion (396).

GENDARME BATTALIONS AND COMMANDS.

1 February 1817– The following *Gendarme battalions* and *Gendarme commands* [*Zhandarmskie diviziony i Zhandarmskiya komandy*] were established, incorporating the Police dragoons [*Politseiskie draguny*] which were located in towns and cities:

Battalions [Diviziony], in the capitals: the *S.-Peterburgskaya* and *Moskovskaya.*

Commands [Komandy], in provincial capitals: *Vologda, Petrozavodsk, Archangel, Novgorod, Pskov, Mitau, Riga, Reval, Vladimir, Kaluga, Kostroma, Orel, Ryazan, Smolensk, Tver, Tula, Yaroslavl, Kiev, Vitebsk, Mogilev, Zhitomir, Kamenets-Podolskii, Minsk, Vilna, Grodno, Bialystok, Yekaterinoslavl, Kursk, Poltava, Simferopol, Kharkov, Kherson, Chernigov, Astrakhan, Nizhnii-Novgorod, Voronezh, Tambov, Vyatka, Kazan, Simbirsk, Penza, Ufa, Perm, Tobolsk, Tomsk,* and *Irkutsk.*

Commands, in port cities: *Theodosia, Taganrog,* and *Odessa.*

Gendarme battalions were subordinate to the Senior Police Chiefs [*Ober-Politsei-meistera*] of the capitals, and were considered as on detached duty from the Corps of the Internal Guard; commands in provincial cities were prescribed to be part of the Garrison battalions in those places, while commands in port towns were part of the Serving Invalid commands (397).

23 February 1817– The *Tsarskoselskaya Zhandarmskaya komanda* was established from the Police Dragoon Command there in Tsarskoe-Selo (398).

3 May 1817– The *Nikolaevskaya Zhandarmskaya komanda* was established in the port town of Nikolaev (399).

31 July 1817– There were established: the *Georgievskaya* and *Saratovskaya Zhandarmskiya komandy* (400).

2 November 1817– There were established: the *Kuopiovskaya* and *Vyborgskaya Zhandarmskiya komandy* (401).

22 November 1817– There were established: the *Tiflisskaya* and *Kishinevskaya Zhandarmskiya komandy* (402).

17 March 1822– The Kuopio Gendarme Command, with its transfer to the city of Helsingfors, was named the *Gelsingforskaya* (403).

12 March 1823– The *Krasnoyarskaya Zhandarmskaya komanda* was established (404).

22 June 1825– The Georgievsk Gendarme Command was transfered to Stavropol and named the *Stavropolskaya* (405).

ARTILLERY GARRISONS

15 April 1805– The Artillery Garrison of the St.-Elizabeth Fortress [*krep. Sv. Yelisavety*] was transferred to Phanagoria and called the Phanagoria Garrison [*Fanagoriiskii Garnizon*], while the Pskov and Velikie-Luki Artillery Garrisons were disbanded (406).

5 July 1808– The *Bombardier Company of the Sveaborg Garrison [Bombardirskaya rota Sveaborgskago Garnizona]* was established, on a field establishment (407).

8 November 1809– Artillery Garrisons in fortresses received numbers and were distributed among 10 regions [*okrugi*]:

   St.-Petersburg Region.

1 company inKronstadt — №1.

½ —— — ——— — № 2.

½ —— — Schlüsselburg — №2.

1 —— — St. Petersburg — №3.

1 —— — Narva — № 4.

1 —— — Novodvinsk — №5.

1 —— — Moscow — №6.

1 —— — Smolensk — №7.

1 —— — Bryansk — №8.

1 —— at the Okhtensk Powder Factory — №9.

   Old Finland [Starofinlyandskii] Region.

1 company in Fredrikshamn — №10.

1 —— — Viborg — №11.

½ —— ——— — №12.

½ —— — Kexholm — №12.

5 companies — Rochensalm — №№13, 15, 16, and 17.

½ company — ——— No. 18.

¼ —— — Villmanstrand — No. 18.

¼ —— — Nyslott — №18.

   New Finland [Novofinlyandskii] Region.

3 companies in Sveaborg — №№19, 20, and 21.

1 company — Gangut FortifiNations — №22.

1 —— — Svartholm — №23.

½ —— — Tavastehus — No. 24.

½ —— — Abo — №24.

   Livonia Region.

2 companies in Riga — №№25 nd 26.

2 —— — Reval — №№27nd 28.

½ company — Dünamünde — №29.

½ —— — Arensburg — №29.

1 company in Pernau — №30.

   Kiev Region.

2 companies in Kiev — №№ 31 and 32.

1 company — Kherson — №33.
1 ———— Kamenets-Podolskii — № 34.
1 ———— Odessa — №35.
½ ———— Tiraspol — №36.
½ ———— Ovidiopol — №36.
½ ———— Kinburn — №37.
½ ———— Ochakov — №37.
2 companies at the Shostensk Powder Factory — №№38 and 39.
  Southern Region.
5 companies in Akhtiar — №№40, 41, 42, 43, and 44.
½ company — Perekop — №45.
½ ———— Phanagoria — №45.
1 ———— Kerch-Yenikale — № 46.
  Astrakhan Region.
1 company in Baku — №47.
½ ———— Derbent — №48.
½ ———— Kizlyar — №48.
1 ———— Astrakhan — №49.
  Caucasus Region.
1 company in Dmitrievsk — №50.
1 ———— Georgievsk — №51.
½ ———— ———— — №52.
½ ———— Azov — №52.
1 ———— Mozdok — №53.
1 ———— Ust-Laba — №54.
1 ———— Kavkazsk — №55.
1 ———— Konstantinogorsk — №56.
½ ———— Tiflis — №57.
½ ———— Yelisavetopol [sic, Yelisavetpol] — №57.
  Orenburg Region.
1 company in Orenburg — №58.
1 ———— Gurev — №59.
1/3 ———— Orsk — №60.
1/3 ———— Kizilsk — №60.
1/3 ———— Verkhne-Uralsk — №60.
1/4 ———— Troitsk — №61.
1/4 ———— Zverinogolovsk — №61.
1 ———— Kazan — №62.
1/2 ———— ——— — №62.
1 company at the Kazan Powder Factory — №63.
  Siberia Region.
1 company in Omsk — №64.
1/4 ———— Yamyshevsk — №65.
1/4 ———— Ust-Kamenogorsk — №65.
1/4 ———— Semipalatinsk — №65.
1/4 ———— Biisk — №65.
3/4 ———— St.-Peter Fortress — №66.
1/4 ———— Zhelezinka — №66.
1/2 ———— Nerchinsk — №67.
1/2 ———— Selenginsk ———
1/2 ———— Irkutsk — №68.
1/2 ———— Petropavlovsk Port — №68.
1 ———— Tobolsk — №69 [408].

5 January 1810– With the inactivation of Gurev's fortress garrison authorization, Artillery Garrison Company №59 [*Artilleriiskaya Garnizonnaya rota №59-go*] which was there was transferred to the fortress at Tatishcheva (409).

31 March 1810– With the inactivation of Schlüsselburg's, Kexholm's, Villmanstrand's, and Azov's fortress garrison authorization, the Artillery Garrison companies at those places were disbanded (410).

14 May 1810– In order to preserve the continuity of numbers after the disbandment of these garrisons, the Kronstadt Artillery garrison was directed to consist of two companies: №№1 and 2; the Viborg Artillery garrison—also of two companies, №№ 11 and 12; the Nyslott Artillery garrison—of half-company №18; and the Georgievsk Artillery garrison—of the two companies №№51 and 52 (411).

15 March 1811– For the fortresses won from the Ottoman Porte: Akkerman, Bendery, Izmail, Kiliya, Braila [*Brailov*], Giurgiu [*Zhurzha*], and Turnu [*Turno*], it was ordered to establish Garrison Artillery companies (412).

23 May 1811– These fortresses, as well as Khotin, captured in the same war, formed a new region [*okrug*] called the *Dunaiskii [Danube]*, and the companies received the following distribution: in Akkerman – 1/4 of Company №70, in Bendery – 3/4 of Company №70, in Izmail – Company №71 and 1/2 of Company №72, in Kiliya – 1/2 of Company №72, in Braila – 3/4 of Company №72, in Giurgiu – 3/4 of Company №73, and in Turnu – 1/4 of Company №73, while Company №34 was transferred to Khotin from Kamenets-Podolskii (413).

9 April 1812– Garrison Artillery Half-company №68, which was stationed at the port of Petropavlovsk, was joined to the 1/2 of Company №68 in Irkutsk, where the entire Company №68 was then located (414).

16 May 1812– The Braila, Giurgiu, and Turnu fortresses were returned to Turkey and consequently the Artillery garrisons located at those places were transferred: from Braila – 1/2 of Company №72 to Izmail and 1/4 of Company №72 to Kiliya, while to Kiev – 3/4 of Company №73 from Giurgiu and 1/4 of Company №73 from Turnu. After this the Danube Region consisted of the following Artillery Garrisons: №34 at Khotin, №70 at Akkerman, №70 at Bendery, №№71 and 72 at Izmail, and №72 at Kiliya (415).

18 May 1812– It was ordered to form Artillery garrisons at those places where there were Artillery reserves: Pskov, Novgorod, Kaluga, and the Shostensk Powder Factory (416).

In 1813– With the inactivation of Ovidiopol's fortress garrison authorization, Artillery Garrison Half-company №36 there was transferred to Tiraspol, where along with the half-company already there it formed Company №36 (417).

5 July 1816– At Zverinogolovsk Fortress, Garrison Artillery Half-company №61 was disbanded, and to preserve the numerical order, the one and a half companies of Company №62, at Kazan, were divided into Half-company №61 and Company № 62 (418).

24 January 1817– The *Georgia [Gruzinskii]* Artillery Region was established, in which were Artillery garrisons: Company №47 at Baku, 1/2 of Company №48 at Derbent, 1/2 of Company №40 at Sukhum-Kale, 1/2 of Company №40 at the St.-Nicholas Fortress [*kr. Sv. Nikolaya*] (both having previously been in Akhtiar), and Company №57 in Tiflis (419).

March 1819– The Astrakhan Artillery Region was abolished and its Artillery garrisons were reassigned to other regions: the Astrakhan garrison, with Garrison Artillery Company №49, – to the Georgia Region, and the Kizlyar garrison – to the Caucasus Region (420).

20 February 1820– Artillery garrisons received a new distribution among the regions and new numbers:

 St.-Petersburg Region.

In St. Petersburg, Company №1, formerly №3, also in St. Petersburg.

— St. Petersburg, ——— №2, formerly №12, also in St. Petersburg.

— Kronstadt, Companies №№3 and 4, formerly №№1 and 2, in Kronstadt.

— Narva, Company №5, formerly №4, in Narva.

— Moscow, Company №6, formerly №6, in Moscow.

— Kaluga, Company №7, newly established.

— Smolensk, Company №8, formerly №7, in Smolensk.

— Bryansk, Company №9, formerly №8, in Bryansk.

— Novodvinsk, Company №10, formerly №5, in Novodvinsk.

At the Okhtensk Powder Factory, Company №11, formerly №9, at the Okhtensk Powder Factory.

 Old Finland Region.

In Fredrikshamn, Company №12, formerly №10, in Fredrikshamn.

— Viborg, №13, formerly №11, in Viborg.

— ——— — 14, formerly №16, in Rochensalm.

— Rochensalm, Company №15, formerly №14, in Rochensalm.

— ——— ——— —16, ——— — 15, — ————

— ——— ——— —17, ——— — 13, — ————

— Nyslott, ½ Company N⁰18, formerly N⁰18, in Nyslott.

— Palois, ½ Company N⁰18, formerly N⁰18, in Rochensalm.

New Finland Region.

In Sveaborg, Company N⁰19, formerly the Sveaborg Bombardier Company.

——— — 20, formerly N⁰19, in Sveaborg.

——— — 21, ——— — 20, — ————

——— — 22, ——— — 21, — ————

— Gangut, Company N⁰23, formerly N⁰22, in Gangut.

— Svartholm, Company N⁰24, formerly N⁰23, in Svartholm.

— Tavastehus, ½ Company N⁰25, formerly N⁰24, in Tavastehus.

— Abo, ½ Company N⁰25, formerly N⁰24, in Abo.

On Aland, Company N⁰26, formerly N⁰17, in Rochensalm.

Livonia Region.

In Riga, Company N⁰27, formerly N⁰26, in Riga.

——— — 28, ——— — 25, — ——

——— — 29, newly established.

— Reval, Company N⁰30, formerly N⁰27, in Reval.

——— — 31, ——— — 28, — ——

— Dünamünde, Company N⁰32, from ½ Company N⁰29, formerly in Dünamünde, and another half-company, newly established.

— Arensburg, Company N⁰33, from Company N⁰29, formerly in Arensburg, and another half-company, newly established.

— Pernau, Company N⁰34, formerly N⁰30, in Pernau.

— Dünaburg, Company N⁰35,newly established.

——— — 36,ditto.

——— — 37, ditto.

— Nesvizh, Company N⁰38, newly established.

— Vilna, Company N⁰39, newly established.

— Grodno, Company N⁰40, newly established.

Kiev Region.

In Kiev, Company N⁰41, formerly N⁰31, in Kiev.

——— — 42, ——— — 32, — ——

——— — 43, ——— — 73, — ——

— Kherson, Company N⁰44, formerly No. 33, in Kherson.

— Bobruisk, Company N⁰45,newly established.

——— — 46, ditto.

——— — 47, ditto.

— Odessa, Company N⁰48, formerly N⁰35, in Odessa.

— Tiraspol, Company N⁰49, formerly N⁰36, in Tiraspol.

— Kinburn, ½ Company N⁰50, formerly N⁰37, in Kinburn.

— Ochakov, ½ Company N⁰50, formerly N⁰37, in Ochakov.

— Modlin, ½ Company N⁰51newly established.

— Zamosc, ½ Company N⁰51.

At the Shostensk Powder Factory, Company N⁰52, formerly N⁰38,formerly at the Shostensk Powder Factory.

——— — 53, ——— — 39, ditto.

Southern Region.

In Akhtiar, Company N⁰54, formerly N⁰41, in Akhtiar.

——— —55, ——— —42, — ——

——— — 56, ——— —43, — ——

——— — 57, ——— — 44, — ——

— Phanagoria, ½ Company N⁰58, formerly N⁰45, in Phanagoria.

— Perekop, ½ Company N⁰58, formerly N⁰45, in Perekop.

— Kerch-Yenikale, Company №59, formerly №46, in Kerch-Yenikale.

Caucasus Region.

In Dimitrievsk Fortress, Company №60, formerly №50, in Dimitrievsk Fortress.

— Georgievsk Fortress, ———   — 61, ———   — 51, in Georgievsk Fortress.

— Georgievsk Fortress, ½ Company №62, formerly №52, in Georgievsk Fortress.

— Kizlyar Fortress, ½ Company №62, formerly №48, in Kizlyar.

Mozdok Fortress, Company №63, formerly №53, in Mozdok.

Ust-Laba Fortress, ———   — 64, ———   — 54, in Ust-Laba.

Kavkazsk Fortress, ———   — 65, ———   — 55, in Kavkazsk.

— Konstantinogorsk Fortress, Company №66, formerly №56, in Konstantinogorsk.

Georgia Region.

In Tiflis, Company №67, formerly №57 in Tiflis, and ½ Company №68, formerly №52 in Georgievsk, later at the St.-Nicholas Fortress.

— Derbent, ½ Company №68, formerly №48, in Derbent.

— Astrakhan, Company №69, formerly №49, in Astrakhan.

— Baku, Company №70, formerly №47, in Baku.

— Sukhum-Kale, ½ Company №71, formerly №40, in Sukhum-Kale.

— St.-Nicholas Fortress, ½ Company №71, formerly №40, at St.-Nicholas Fortress.

Orenburg Region.

In Orenburg, Company №72, formerly №57, in Orenburg.

— Tatishcheva Fortress, Company №73, formerly №59, at Tatishcheva Fortress.

— Orsk, Company №74, formerly №60, in Orsk.

— Troitsk, ½ Company №75, formerly №61, in Troitsk.

— Kazan, ½ Company №75, formerly №61, in Kazan.

— ———   Company №76, formerly №62, in Kazan.

At the Kazan Powder Factory, Company №77, formerly №63, at the Kazan Powder Factory.

Siberia Region.

In Tobolsk, Company №78, formerly №69, in Tobolsk.

— Omsk, Company №79, formerly №64, at Omsk.

— Irkutsk, Company №80, formerly №68, in Irkutsk.

— Selenginsk, ½ Company №81, formerly №67, in Selenginsk.

— Nerchinsk, ½ Company №81, formerly №67, at Nerchinsk.

— St.-Peter Fortress, 3/4 Company №82, formerly №66, at the St.-Peter Fortress.

— Zhelezinka, 1/4 Company №82, formerly №66, in Zhelezinka.

— Ust-Kamenogorsk, 1/4 Company №83, formerly №65, in Ust-Kamenogorsk.

— Yamyshevo, 1/4 Company №83, formerly №65, in Yamyshevo.

— Biisk, 1/4 Company №83, formerly №65, in Biisk.

— Semipalatinsk, 1/4 Company №83, formerly №65, in Semipalatinsk.

Danube Region.

In Khotin, Company №84, formerly №34, in Khotin.

— Bendery, 3/4 Company №85, formerly №70, at Bendery.

— Akkerman, 1/4 Company №85, formerly №70, in Akkerman.

— Izmail,   Company №86, formerly №71, in Izmail.

— —— ½ Company №87, formerly №72, in Izmail.

— Kiliya, ½ Company №87, formerly №72, at Kiliya.

— Kamenets-Podolskii, Company №88, newly established [421].

27 June 1820– Garrison Artillery Half-company №58, in Phanagoria, was reassigned to the Caucasus Region [422].

27 November 1820– With the disestablishment of the St.-Nicholas Fortress, Half-company №71 there was transferred to the Redut-Kale fortification [423].

23 March 1822– Garrison Artillery Company №44, in Kherson, was reassigned to the Southern Region [424].

11 February 1825– Garrison Artillery Company №48 in Odessa was disbanded [425], and subsequently there were no further changes in Artillery garrisons during 1825.

Besides the Artillery garrisons enumerated here, during the latter part of Emperor Alexander I's reign there were the following establishments as part of the Artillery Department [*Artilleriiskoe vedomstvo*]:

   a.) *Permanent arsenals [Nepremennye arsenaly]:* the *S.-Peterburgskii, Bryanskii, Kievskii,* and *Kazanskii.*

   b.) *Mobile arsenals [Podvizhnye arsenaly]:* №№1, 2, and 3; the last was with the 2nd Army, and the first two—with the 1st Army.

   c.) *Powder factories [Porokhovye zavody]:* the *Okhtenskii, Shostenskii,* and *Kazanskii.*

   d.) *Arms factories [Oruzheinye zavody]:* the *Tulskii [Tula], Izhevskii,* and *Sestroretskii.*

   e.) *The Moscow Artillery Depot [Moskovskoe Artilleriiskoe Depo]* (426).

ENGINEER COMMANDS

25 August 1808– *Engineer Commands [Inzhenernyya komandy]* were established in the newly won fortresses: Sveaborg, Gangut, or Gangeud, Kronenburg, Svartholm, and Kyumengorod (427).

11 October 1809– With the Engineer Department's new organization and the distribution of all fortresses among 10 regions [*okrugi*], Engineer commands received the following apportionment:

   Novofinlyandskii [New Finland] Okrug – Sveaborgskaya, Gangeudskaya, Kronenburgskaya, Svartgolmskaya [Svartholm], Rochensalmskaya, Kyumenegorodskaya, and Fridrikhsgamskaya [Fredrikshamn].

   Starofinlyandskii [Old Finland] Okrug– Vyborgskaya [Viborg], Vilmanstrandskaya [Villmanstrand], Neishlotskaya [Nyslott], and Keksgolmskaya [Kexholm].

   S.-Peterburgskii Okrug – S.-Peterburgskaya, Kronshtadtskaya [Kronstadt], Shlisselburgskaya [Schlüsselburg], and Arkhangelsko-Novodvinskaya [Archangel-Novodvinsk].

   Liflyandskii [Livonia] Okrug– Narvskaya [Narva], Revelskaya [Reval], Pernovskaya [Pernau], Arensburgskaya, Rizhskaya [Riga], and Dinamindskaya [Dünamünde].

   Kievskii Okrug– Kamenets-Podolskaya, Kievskaya, Tiraspolskaya, Ovidiopolskaya, Odesskaya [Odessa], Dmitrievskaya, and Azovskaya.

   Khersonskii Okrug– Khersonskaya, Kinburnskaya, Nikolaevskaya (at Ochakov), Perekopskaya, Akhtiarskaya, Kerchenskaya, Yenikolskaya [Yenikale], and Fanagoriiskaya [Phanagoria].

   Kavkazskii [Caucasus] Okrug– Ust-Labinskaya [Ust-Laba], Kavkazskaya, Temolesskaya, Georgievskaya, Mozdokskaya, and Kizlyarskaya.

   Astrakhanskii Okrug– Bakinskaya [Baku], Derbentskaya, Tsaritsynskaya, Chernoyarskaya [Chernyi-Yar], Yenotaevskaya, and Gurevskaya.

   Orenburgskii Okrug – Orenburgskaya, Kalmykovskaya, Orskaya, Kizilskaya, Verkhneuralskaya [Verkhne-Uralsk], Troitskaya, and Zverinogolovskaya.

   Sibirskii [Siberia] Okrug – Petrovskaya, Omskaya, Ust-Kamenogorskaya, Yamyshevskaya, Semipalatinskaya, Biiskaya, Kuznetskaya [428].

5 January 1810– With the disestablishment of the Gurev Fortress, the Engineer command there was disbanded (429).

31 March 1810– With the disestablishment of the Schlüsselburg, Villmanstrand, Kexholm, Azov, Chernyi-Yar, and Yenotaevsk fortresses, the Engineer commands at those places were disbanded, and consequent to this, the Rochensalm, Kyumenegorod, and Fredrikshamn Engineer Commands were reassigned to the Old Finland Region (430).

9 February 1811– Engineer officers were granted rank privileges the same as those given to the Field Art. at this same time (431).

23 May 1811– With the establishment of the *Danube [Dunaiskii]* Engineer Region from the fortresses won from Turkey: Khotin, Bendery, Izmail, Akkerman, Kiliya, Braila, Giurgiu, and Turnu, there were established Engineer commands at these places, and for the first of these the command was transferred from Kamenets-Podolskii (432).

16 May 1812– The last three fortresses were returned to Turkey, and consequently the Engineer commands which had been there were disbanded. In this same year the Olviopol Engineer Command was disbanded and a new one formed, the *Bobruiskaya* (433).

5 July 1816– The *Dünaburg* Engineer Command was established, unassigned to any region, and the Kronenburg was disbanded (434).

3 April 1818– The Kyumenegorod and Ochakov, or Nikolaev, Engineer Commands were disbanded (435).

1 January 1819– Engineer field and company-grade officers [*shtab i ober-ofitsery*] were divided as either *Field [Polevoi]* or *Garrison [Garizonnyi]*, of which the first maintained the rank privileges granted on 9 February, 1811, while the latter were not given these privileges. The Astrakhan Engineer Region was abolished and all Engineer commands received a new distribution among 10 regions:

   New Finland Region – Sveaborg, Gangeud, and Svartgolm.

   Old Finland Region– Viborg, Fredrikshamn, Rochensalm, and Nyslott.

   St.-Petersburg Region – St.-Petersburg, Kronstadt, Narva, and Archangel-Novodvinsk.

Livonia Region– Riga, Dünaburg, Reval,Pernau,and Arensburg.
Kiev Region– Kiev,Odessa,and Dmitrievsk.
Danube Region– Bendery,Khotin,Izmail, andKiliya.
Kherson Region– Kherson,Kinburn,Perekop,Akhtiar,Yenikale, andPhanagoria.
Georgia Region– Georgievsk,Tiflis,Astrakhan,Derbent,Baku, Kizlyar, Mozdok,andKavkazsk.
Orenburg Region – Orenburg andOrsk.
Siberia Region – Omsk, Petropavlovsk,and Ust-Kamenogorsk.

Commands in the list of 11 December, 1809, but which are not shown in this table, were disbanded (436).

14 June 1820– The *Alandskaya Inzhenernaya komanda* was established in the New Finland Region (437).

27 June 1820– The Phanagoria Engineer Command was reassigned from the Kherson Region to the Georgia Region (438).

11 February 1825– With the disestablishment of the Odessa Fortress, its Engineer command was disbanded, and in this same year the Kavkazsk Command was also disbanded (439).

28 June 1825– With the Georgievsk no longer one of the authorized fortresses, the Engineer command there was disbanded (440), and afterwards there were no further changes in the number or distribution of Engineer commands during the reign of Emperor Alexander I.

Besides the commands listed in this overview, there were also under the Engineer Department: two Siege [*Osadnyi*] and two Field [*Polevoi*] Replacement Engineer Parks [*Zapasnye Inzhenernye Parki*], established on 16 December, 1821, using equipment, transport, and other materiel left as surplus after the organizational changes in the Sapper and Pioneer battalions, as well as from equipment and reserves of the Engineer Depots (441).

MILITARY LABOR ANDCRAFTSMEN BATTALIONS AND COMPANIES

27 September 1807– With the abolishment of the Land Militia [*Zemskaya Militia*], formed in 1806, those of its soldiers [*ratniki*] who proved to be unfit for field service were turned to the carrying out of fortification work (442).

25 November 1807– These soldiers were called *Military Laborers [Voennye rabochie]* (443).

2 May 1816– The two, four-company, battalions established for works by the Moscow Commission of Construction [*Moskovskaya Kommissiya stroenii*] were called the 1st and 2nd Labor Battalions [*Rabochie Bataliony*] (444).

11 April 1817– There were established the 1st and 2nd *Military Labor Battalions [Voenno-rabochie bataliony]* of the Department of Lines of Communications [*vedomstvo Putei Soobshcheniya*], each of one craftsmen [*masterovaya*] company and three labor companies (445).

11 February 1818– A *Craftsmen Battalion [Masterovaya batalion]*, of four craftsmen companies, was established for building regimental headquarters in the Military Settlements and homes for military settlers (446).

29 June 1818– The 1st and 2nd Moscow Labor Battalions were ordered to be named *Military Labor Battalions №№1and 2*; the Military Labor Battalions of the Lines of Communications became *Military Labor Battalions №№3and 4*; and the Craftsmen Battalion in the Military Settlement became *Military Labor Battalion №5*(447).

19 August 1818– In place of the invalids who had been with the Survey Chancellery [*Mezhevaya Kantselyariya*] and its Offices [*kontory*], there was formed the four-company *Military Labor Battalion №6*, and in the Novgorod Military Settlement there was established *Military Labor Battalion №7*(448).

21 August 1818– In place of the craftsmen, military laborers, and train personnel on Engineer Department projects, there were established *Military Labor Companies, from № 1 to №36*, inclusive (449).

18 December 1818– A *Temporary Military Labor Company [Vremennaya Voenno-rabochaya rota]* was established in the city of Tiflis to carry out state projects (450).

2 February 1820– Two *Military Labor companies* were established at the Tula Arms Factory (451).

29 April 1820– These companies were ordered to be called *Military Labor Companies №№37and 38*, and were considered part of the Garrison Artillery (452).

3 December 1820– Four more *Military Labor Companies №№39, 40, 41, and 42* were established, designated for work at the barracks of the Guards forces (453).

22 February 1821– In Tiflis, in addition to the single temporary Military Labor company established there in 1817, there was formed an additional such company (454).

23 March 1822– Military Labor Companies №№37 and 38 were reassigned to the Engineer Department (455).

7 June 1823– From Military Labor Battalion №8, located in the Military Settlements of Kherson, Yekaterinoslavl, and Slobodsko-Ukraine provinces, there were formed two Military Labor battalions: №7for the Slobodsko-Ukraine Military

Settlements, and №8for the Kherson and Yekaterinoslavl Settlements. After this, Military Labor Battalion №7 in the Novgorod Military Settlement became *№6*, and the former *№6* was assigned *№9* (456).

9 August 1823– The *Craftsmen Company of the Headquarters of HIS IMPERIAL MAJESTY [Masterovaya rota Glavnago Shtaba EGO IMPERATORSKAGO VELICHESTVA]* was established for the Court Carriage Establishment [*Pridvornoe Ekipazhnoe zavedenie*] (457).

By 1826 the distribution of Military Labor battalions and companies was as follows:

a) *Military Labor battalions:*

№№1 and 2 – in Moscow; №№3 and 4 – with the Department of Lines of Communications; №№5, 6, 7, 8, and one company of №9 – with the Separate Corps of Military Settlements, and the other three companies of №9 – with the Survey Department.

b) *Military Labor companies:*

№№1, 2, 3, and 4 – in the New Finland Engineering Region; №№5 and 6 – in the Old Finland Region; №№7, 8, and 9 – in the St.-Petersburg Region, №№11, 12, 13, 14, 15, 16, 17, and 18 – in the Livonia Region; №№19, 20, 21, 22, 23, 24, and 25 – in the Kiev Region, №№26, 27, 28, and 37 – in the Danube Region; №№29, 30, 31, and 38 – in the Kherson Region, №№32, 33, and 34 – in the Georgia Region; №№35 – in the Orenburg Region; №№36 – in the Siberia Region; and №№39, 40, 41, and 42 – with the Guards Barracks Commission [*Gvardeiskaya Kazarmennaya Kommissiya*]. In addition there were still the two Temporary Military Labor Companies №№1 and 2 with the Separate Caucasus Corps.

The Craftsmen Company of the Headquarters of HIS IMPERIAL MAJESTYwas, as before, with the Court Carriage Establishment (458).

NOTES

(310) PSZ, Vol. XXVIII, pp. 3, 4 and 240, No. No. 21,114, 21,115, and 21,240, and above, in the description of garrisons, entry for 30 April, 1802.
(311) Chronicle of Garrison regiments and battalions, held in the Archive of the Inspection Department of the Ministry of War, pg. 34.
(312) PSZ, Vol. XXVIII, pg. 489, No. 21,930.
(313) Chronicle of Garrison regiments and battalions, held in the Archive of the Inspection Department of the Ministry of War.
(314) PSZ, Vol. XXX, pg. 763, No. 23,447.
(315) PSZ, Vol. XXX, pg. 93, No. 23,568.
(316) PSZ, Vol. XXX, pg. 952, No. 23,629.
(317) PSZ, Vol. XXX, pg. 1,353, No. 24,007.
(318) PSZ, Vol. XXXI, pp. 16 and 19, No. No. 24,068 and 24,070.
(319) PSZ, Vol. XXXI, pg. 395, No. 24,487.
(320) PSZ, Vol. XXXI, pg. 593, No. 24,568.
(321) See this date for Mobile Invalid companies.
(322) PSZ, Vol. XXXIII, pg. 1,013, No. 26,426.
(323) See this date for Mobile Invalid companies.
(324) Ibid.
(325) PSZ, Vol. XXXI, pg. 593, No. 24,568.
(326) PSZ, Vol. XXXI, pg. 809, No. 24,712.
(327) PSZ, Vol. XXXI, pg. 846, No. 24,781.
(328) PSZ, Vol. XXXV, pg. 120, No. 27,279.
(329) PSZ, Vol. XXXII, pg. 173, No. 24,979.
(330) PSZ, Vol. XXXIII, pg. 597, No. 26,219, and List of forces for 1816.
(331) PSZ, Vol. XXXIII, pg. 957, No. 26,370.
(332) PSZ, Vol. XXXIII, pg. 1,013, No. 26,426, and pg. 1,042, No. 26,453.
(333) PSZ, Vol. XXXIII, pg. 1,061, No. 26,490.
(334) List of forces for 1818.
(335) PSZ, Vol. XXXIV, pg. 413, No. 26,937.
(336) List of forces for 1817.
(337) PSZ, Vol. XXXV, pg. 71, No. 27,238.
(338) PSZ, Vol. XXXV, pg. 420, No. 27,456.
(339) PSZ, Vol. XXXV, pg. 617, No. 27,577.
(340) PSZ, Vol. XXXVI, pg. 61, No. 27,672.
(341) Highest confirmed List of Mobile Invalid companies, 3 March, 1819.
(342) PSZ, Vol. XXXVI, pg. 406, No. 28,013; Vol. XXXVIII, pg. 1,181, No. 29,589; and List of forces for 1825.
(343) List of forces for 1825.
(344) PSZ, Vol. XXXI, pg. 593, №24,568.

(345) PSZ, Vol. XXXI, pg. 931, No. 24,923.

(346) Highest confirmed Administrative Decree for Guards Mobile Invalid companies, 31 December, 1815.

(347) PSZ, Vol. XXXIII, pg. 933, No. 26,350.

(348) PSZ, Vol. XXXIII, pg. 1,013, No. 26,426.

(349) PSZ, Vol. XXXIII, pg. 1,057, No. 26,479.

(350) PSZ, Vol. XXXIII, pg. 1,091, No. 21,517.

(351) PSZ, Vol. XXXIV, pg. 102, No. 26,721.

(352) PSZ, Vol. XXXIV, pg. 257, No. 26,830.

(353) PSZ, Vol. XXXIV, pg. 325, No. 26,891.

(354) PSZ, Vol. XXXVI, pg. 233, No. 27,838.

(355) PSZ, Vol. XXXVI, pg. 465, No. 28,442.

(356) PSZ, Vol. XXXVII, pg. 806, No. 28,726.

(357) Order of the Chief of HIS IMPERIAL MAJESTY'S Headquarters, 10 September, 1821, No. 56.

(358) PSZ, Vol. XXXVIII, pg. 201, No. 29,042.

(359) PSZ, Vol. XXXVIII, pg. 699, No. 29,254.

(360) PSZ, Vol. XXXVIII, pg. 711, No. 29,266.

(361) Order to the Separate Corps of Military Settlements, 19 April, 1823.

(362) PSZ, Vol. XXXVIII, pg. 1,181, No. 29,588.

(363) PSZ, Vol. XXXIX, pg. 254, No. 29,863, where, as a misprint, Tambov appears in place of Tomsk.

(364) PSZ, Vol. XXXIX, pg. 437, No. 29,983.

(365) PSZ, Vol. XXXIX, pg. 642, No. 30,140.

(366) List of the Internal Guard for 1825.

(367) Ibid.

(368) PSZ, Vol. XXXIV, pg. 288, No. 26,847.

(369) List of étapes for 1817.

(370) PSZ, Vol. XXXIV, pg. 486, No. 27,006.

(371) PSZ, Vol. XXXV, pg. 61, No. 27,224.

(372) PSZ, Vol. XXXV, pg. 84, No. 27,255.

(373) PSZ, Vol. XXXV, pg. 95, No. 27,265.

(374) List of forces for 1818.

(375) PSZ, Vol. XXXVI, pg. 191, No. 27,800.

(376) PSZ, Vol. XXXVII, pp. 22 and 23, No. №28,104 and 28,105.

(377) Highest confirmed List of étapes from Moscow to the city of Aleksandrov, 1 April, 1821.

(378) Report of the Commander of the Separate Corps of the Internal Guard to the Chief of HIS IMPERIAL MAJESTY'S Headquarters, from 25 May, 1821, No. 899, with a Highest resolution of 1 June, 1821.

(379) PSZ, Vol. XXXVII, pg. 84, No. 28,935.

(380) PSZ, Vol. XXXVIII, pp. 337 and 338, No. 29,118.

(381) PSZ, Vol. XXXVIII, pp. 469 and 481, №29,129.

(382) PSZ, Vol. XXXVIII, pg. 629, №28,198.

(383) PSZ, Vol. XXXVIII, pg. 639, No. 28,204.

(384) Highest Order, announced by the Duty Officer of HIS IMPERIAL MAJESTY'S Headquarters, from 2 December, 1822, (in the correspondence of the Inspection Department of the IInd Section, No. 4,738, on reviewing the General Compilation of Military Regulations, 1830).

(385) PSZ, Vol. XXXVIII, pg. 699, No. 28,254.

(386) Correspondence of the Acting Quartermaster-General of HIS IMPERIAL MAJESTY'S Headquarters to the Duty General of this Headquarters, from 1 December, 1823, under No. 458.

(387) Similar correspondence from 12 January, 1824, under No. 7.

(388) PSZ, Vol. XXXIX, pg. 185, No. 29,820, and List of étape commands.

(389) PSZ, Vol. XXXIX, pg. 306, No. 29,897.

(390) List of étapes for 1824 and 1825.

(391) PSZ, Vol. XL, pg. 52, No. 30,210.

(392) PSZ, Vol. XL, No. 20,415.

(393) List of forces for 1825.

(394) Signed Order to the Chief of HIS IMPERIAL MAJESTY'S Headquarters, from 12 August, 1818, and List of forces for 1818.

(395) Signed Order to the Chief of HIS IMPERIAL MAJESTY'S Headquarters, from 12 August, 1818, and List of forces for 1818.

(396) Signed Order to the Chief of HIS IMPERIAL MAJESTY'S Headquarters, from 23 April 1819, and List of forces for 1819.

(397) PSZ, Vol. XXXIV, pg. 50, No. 26,650.

(398) PSZ, Vol. XXXIV, pg. 83, No. 26,692.

(399) Correspondence of the Inspection Department, III Sect., 1817, No. 36, on the establishment of Gendarme commands in provincial capitals.

(400) PSZ, Vol. XXXIV, pg. 461, No. 26,980.

(401) PSZ, Vol. XXXIV, pg. 860, No. 27,126.

(402) PSZ, Vol. XXXIV, pg. 884, No. 27,155.

(403) Correspondence of the Inspection Department, II Sect. 16 February, 1822, No. 189, on the disbandment of the Kuopio Gendarme Command.

(404) PSZ, Vol. XXXVIII, pg. 826, No. 29,353.

(405) PSZ, Vol. XL, pg. 333, No. 30,391.

(406) PSZ, Vol. XXVIII, pg. 981, No. 21,715.

(407) PSZ, Vol. XLIII, part 2, pg. 68, No. 23,142.

(408) Highest confirmed List of Artillery Garrison companies, 8 November, 1809.

(409) PSZ, Vol. XXXI, pg. 16, No. 24,069, and Highest confirmed List of Artillery Garrison companies by regions, 20 February, 1820.

(410) PSZ, Vol. XXXI, pg. 104, No. 24,173.

(411) PSZ, Vol. XXXI, pg. 183, No. 24,229.

(412) PSZ, Vol. XXXI, pg. 579, No. 24,557.

(413) PSZ, Vol. XXXI, pg. 659, No. 24,643, and assignments of companies. See, in the Archive of the Inspection Department of the Ministry of War, Book with List of Artillery for various years beginning in 1797.

(414) PSZ, Vol. XXXII, pg. 282, No. 25,081, §§ 15 and 16, and the Archive of the Inspection Department of the Ministry of War, Book with List of Artillery for various years beginning in 1797.

(415) PSZ, Vol. XXXII, pg. 316, No. 25,110, and the List referred to in the above note.

(416) PSZ, Vol. XXXII, pg. 322, No. 25,112.

(417) Archive of the Inspection Department of the Ministry of War, Book with List of Artillery for various years beginning in 1797.

(418) List of forces for 1816 and 1817, Archive of the Inspection Department of the Ministry of War No. №3 and 5.

(419) PSZ, Vol. XXXIV, pg. 34, No. 26,636, and List of forces for 1817, Archive of the Inspection Department of the Ministry of War No. 5.

(420) PSZ, Vol. XXXVI, pg. 130, No. 27,749.

(421) Highest confirmed List of Artillery Garrison companies, 20 February, 1820.

(422) PSZ, Vol. XXXVII, pg. 372, No. 28,333, and Highest confirmed List of Forces, 23 March, 1822.

(423) PSZ, Vol. XXVII [sic], pg. 516, No. 28,473.

(424) Highest confirmed List of Forces, 23 March, 1822.

(425) PSZ, Vol. XL, pg. 60, No. 30,222.

(426) List of forces for 1825.

(427) PSZ, Vol. XXX, pg. 550, No. 23,251.

(428) PSZ, Vol. XXX, pg. 1,204, No. 23,902, and Vol. XLIII, part II, sect. I, pp. 259 and 263, No. 23,902.

(429) PSZ, Vol. XXX, pg. 16, No. 24,049.

(430) PSZ, Vol. XXXI, pg. 104, No. 24,173, and List of forces for 1810.

(431) Highest Order.

(432) PSZ, Vol. XXXI, pg. 659, No. 24,643, and Lists of forces for 1811 and 1812.

(433) PSZ, Vol. XXXIII, pg. 316, No. 25,210, and Lists of forces for 1812 and 1813.

(434) List of forces from 5 July, 1816, through 1 July, 1817.

(435) List of forces for 1819.

(436) PSZ, Vol. XXXVI, pp. 3 and 5, No. 27,617.

(437) Highest confirmed List of forces, 14 June, 1820.

(438) PSZ, Vol. XXXVII, pg. 372, No. 28,333.

(439) PSZ, Vol. XL, pg. 60, No. 30,222, and List of forces for 1825.

(440) PSZ, Vol. XL, pg. 340, No. 30,396, and List of forces for 1825.

(441) PSZ, Vol. XLIII, part II, sect. 1, pp. 197 and 198, No. 28,836.

(442) PSZ, Vol. XXIX, pg. 1,294, №22,636.

(443) Collection of Laws and Directives, 1835, Book IV, pg. 51.

(444) List of forces for the year 1836.

(445) Papers of the Inspection Department of the War Ministry, 2nd Sect., 3rd Office, for No 163, pt. 5, pp. 214-220, and list of battalions of the Internal Guard.

(446) Collection of Laws and Directives, 1839, Book II, pg. 67, and list of battalions of the Internal Guard.

(447) Papers in the Archive of the Inspection Department of the War Ministry, 2nd Sect., 3rd Office, for No 163, pt. 7, pp. 535 et seq., and list of battalions of the Internal Guard.

(448) Order of the Minister of War, 16 April 1843, No 50.

(449) Ibid., 27 March 1847, No 51.

(450) Ibid., 13 April 1847, No 61.

(451) Ibid., 18 July 1849, No 65.

(452) Ibid., 28 September 1850, No 68.

(453) Ibid., 12 March 1852.

(454) PSZ, Vol. XXXVII, pg. 629, No. 28,561.

(455) Highest confirmed List of forces, 23 March, 1822.

(456) PSZ, Vol. XXXVIII, pg. 1,029, No. 29,500.

(457) PSZ, Vol. XXXVIII, pg. 1,162, No. 29,578.

(458) List of forces for 1825.

XI ARMY SAPPERS AND PIONEERS (ARMEISKIE SAPERY I PIONERY)

9 April 1801- Lower ranks of the Pioneer Regiment were ordered to cut off their **curls** [*pukli*] and have **queues** [*kosy*] only 7 inches long [*4 vershka*], tying them midway down the collar (184).

27 March 1802– The **Pioneer Regiment** was given the same uniform as that established at this time for Foot Field Artillery, except with white buttons and gray shoulder straps and, for lower ranks, gray breeches (Illus. 1697 and 1698) (185).

27 October 1802- While on the march with troops or on detached duties, Pioneer Generals and field and company-grade officers were ordered to wear, instead of white pants [*pantalony*], gray **riding trousers** [*reituzy*], with bright buttons the same color as those on the coat, and leather lining, as was established at this time for officers of Army Infantry and Cavalry (186).

6 September 1803– The 1st Pioneer Regiment was ordered to have red **shoulder straps**, and the 2nd Regiment—white (187).

17 December 1803– A new table of **uniforms, accouterments, and weaponry** for **Pioneer regiments** was confirmed, based on which private miners, sappers, and pioneers [*ryadovye minery, sapery i pionery*], kept the same uniforms as laid down on 27 March 1802 and 6 September 1803, except that the tricorn hat was replaced by a black cloth shako with a leather visor, similar to the shakos introduced in this same year in Musketeer regiments and the Foot Field Artillery, but with white buttons. The lower tuft or pompon and small upper plume for miners and sappers was red, and white for pioneers (Illus. 1699). Weapons and accouterments included: short sword [*tesak*] of the same pattern as used during the previous tsar's reign; sword knot in company colors, as in Grenadier and Musketeer regiments; whitened infantry sword belt; pistol with brass mountings; black leather pouch [*podsumka*] with a round brass plate on which was the raised image of a two-headed eagle (Illus. 1699). All these ranks were prescribed the same round knapsacks and water flasks as in the infantry (Illus. 1699), but for entrenching work they were issued raven's duck smocks [*ravenduchnye kiteli*] with covered buttons.

Noncommissioned officers, including first sergeants [*fel'dfebeli*], did not carry pistols or wear pouches and smocks. On their coats' collars and cuffs, as well as along the upper edge of the shako, they had silver galloon lace. Following the example of noncommissioned officers in the Army Infantry and Foot Artillery, they were authorized gloves, canes, and the same colored rings [*trinchiki*] on the sword knot and the tuft [*kist'*] on shakos that these ranks had (Illus. 1700).

Company drummers had the exact same chevrons sewn onto the coat and drums as prescribed for drummers in the Army Infantry and Foot Artillery, but with black drumsticks (Illus. 1700).

Battalion drummers also had chevrons and drums of the same patterns as used by battalion drummers in the Army Infantry and Foot Artillery, as well as the same noncommissioned-officer gloves, canes, shako tufts, sword knots, and galloon lace as they had, except the lace was silver (Illus. 1701).

Field and company-grade officers kept the uniforms they had received on 27 March and 27 October 1801, except the hats were ordered to be worn with a tall plume and a button loop of narrow silver galloon (Illus. 1702). Shabracks and holsters were authorized for them as in the Foot Field Artillery, but with silver galloon.

Generals were distinguished from field-grade officers only by their hats with white plumage (Illus. 1702).

Noncombatant lower ranks—namely wagon masters, medical assistants, clerks, barbers, lazarette orderlies, master craftsmen, and train personnel—had all the same uniforms, accouterments, and weaponry as corresponding ranks in the Foot Artillery, with just the gold galloon (used by noncommissioned officer ranks) changed to silver, and yellow metal buttons to white.

Doctors [*lekarya*] were uniformed exactly as doctors in other branches (188).

1 July 1806– There were the same changes in uniforms of **doctors** as described in detail above for Grenadier regiments (189).

1 October 1806 – The **sheepskin warm coats** [*ovchinnyya fufaiki*] authorized for lower ranks up to now were withdrawn (190).

2 December 1806– Lower ranks were ordered to cut their **hair** short. Generals, though, and field and company-grade officers, were in this regard allowed to proceed according to their personal wishes (191).

10 March 1807– **Canes** were withdrawn for officers and noncommissioned officers (192).

23 December 1807– Lower ranks were given new pattern summer and winter **pants** of the pattern confirmed at this same time for Grenadier and Musketeer regiments, i.e. with spats for the first, and for the second—leather trim or leggings [*kragi*], with seven brass buttons. Along with this, privates were directed to exchange their small pouches [*podsumki*] for **pouches** [*sumy*] on a crossbelt over the left shoulder, as established for Army Infantry regiments (193).

3 January 1808– Generals and field and company-grade officers of Pioneer regiments were ordered to have **epaulettes** on their coats of the same pattern as that established at this same time for generals and officers of the Foot Field Artillery, except with silver trim instead of gold (Illus. 1703). Lower ranks were told to have worsted cord numbers sewn onto their **shoulder straps**, in yellow for the 1st Regiment and in red for the 2nd (Illus. 1703) (194).

26 January 1808– Generals of Pioneer regiments were ordered to wear the newly established standard pattern general officer's coat during parades, on official holidays [*tabel'nye dni*], and at all gatherings of troops, in peacetime as well as during war. With the regimental uniform off duty, they were to have dark-green pants instead of white (195).

7 March 1808– Sword belts [*portupei*] in Pioneer regiments were ordered to be worn not around the waist but over the right shoulder, as described for Grenadier and Musketeer regiments (196). From this same time the cloth **shakos** introduced in 1803 began to be lined with black leather to make them stronger, and the visors for them were sewn on. After this they received the name of *kiver* (Illus. 1703) (197).

14 July 1808 – For lower ranks of Pioneer regiments the round **knapsacks** were exchanged for rectangular ones of the same pattern as those established at this time for Grenadier and Musketeer regiments. Along with it was set forth as a rule for these personnel to carry the **greatcoat**, when it was not being worn, in accordance with the rules set forth above for Grenadiers (Illus. 1703) coat (198).

2 November 1808– The **pants** authorized on 23 December 1807, with leggings in the winter and spats in the summer, were kept only for combatant lower ranks, while for noncombatants the pants as well as the boots were directed to be of the patterns established on 17 December 1803 (199).

5 November 1808– Company-grade officers of Pioneer regiments, when the troops were wearing **knapsacks**, were ordered to also have them, of the same pattern in all respects as was established for lower ranks (200).

12 November 1808– Field and company-grade officers, when not on duty, were allowed to wear dark-green cloth **pants** instead of white ones (201).

11 February 1809– All **noncombatant lower ranks** except those holding noncommissioned officer status were given a new pattern **cap** [*shapka*] in place of the shako and forage cap with tassel, identical to those which were introduced at this time in Army Infantry regiments, but with a black band and red piping around its edges (202).

4 April 1809- **Noncommissioned officers** were ordered to have **galloon** not on the lower and side edges of the collar, but on the upper and side edges (Illus. 1704) (203).

20 April 1809 – The change in the manner of wearing the **knapsack**, introduced at this time for Army Infantry, i.e. with the addition of a third strap running crossways over the chest, was also adopted for Pioneer regiments (Illus. 1704) (204).

8 June 1809–The plumage on **generals' hats** was discontinued and the former pattern of buttonhole was replaced with a new one made of four thick, twisted cords, of which the two middle ones were intertwined with each other as if in a plait (205).

17 October 1809– Lower ranks were ordered to have yellow (brass) buttons at the bottom of their pants on the leather **leggings**, instead of white (Illus. 1704) (206).

18 November 1809– Lower ranks were ordered to have a small bomb and cords on their **shakos**: the first of the pattern used by musketeers except in white, and the latter of the style for artillery, i.e. red for privates and drummers, and white with black and orange for noncommissioned officers and musicians (Illus. 1704). Miners' pompons [*repeiki*] were red, sappers' were white, and pioneer's were white with a dark-green center (Illus. 1705) (207).

6 December 1809– Field and company-grade officers of Pioneer regiments were ordered to wear a **shako** [*kiver*] instead of the hat when in formation, of the same pattern as established at this time for Musketeer officers, only with white fittings (Illus. 1706), but when not in formation the hat was kept as before except now with a shortened plume (208).

In this same year the **powdering of the hair** was completely discontinued for officers, and it was permitted for them when off duty to wear **frock coats** like the officers' frock coats in the Army infantry, except with black collar and cuffs piped red, black lining, and white buttons (209).

24 September 1810- **Knapsack straps** were ordered to be stitched on the edges, in the manner of crossbelts and sword belts, and have a bend at each shoulder so that they do wear away the coat and constrict a man under his arms (210).

17 January 1811– Instead of the multicolored **cords** on their **shakos**, noncommissioned officers and musicians were ordered to have white ones, with only the tassels beint tricolored: white, black, and orange (211).

5 February 1811– Company-grade officers were ordered to wear dark-green **pants** on all occasions (212).

22 February 1811 – Instead of white **shako cords**, noncommissioned officers and musicians were ordered to have red ones with multicolored tassels (213).

25 October 1811– Lower ranks were given dark-green **forage caps** of a new pattern, with red piping and a black band on which was to be sewn the company number in white cord(214).

3 November 1811- **Gloves** were abolished for noncommissioned officers, and to replace them in cold weather they were allowed to wear cloth mittens sewn from old dress coats, as done at this time by privates (215).

17 December 1811- **Noncombatant lower ranks** were given new uniforms identical to those received at this time by noncombatant lower ranks of the Foot Field Artillery, but with white buttons for privates and silver galloon lace for noncommissioned officers(216).

10 February 1812- Noncombatant lower ranks were ordered to have **shoulder straps** of the same color and pattern as the shoulder straps of combatant lower ranks (217), and about this time there were the following changes in the uniforms of combatant ranks:

1) New-pattern **shakos** were issued, with a big indentation or widening upwards, and sloping upwards at the sides. They now lacked the sewn-on neck flaps or ear flaps, which from this time on were worn separately (Illus. 1707).   2) The high **collars** which opened diagonally upwards were replaced by lower ones closed with small hooks (Illus. 1707).

3) Lower combatant ranks were given **gaiters** [*kragi*] and officers **high boots** reaching up to the knees, the first having nine buttons (Illus. 1707).

4) In order to lessen their expenditures, officers were allowed to have **white shako cords, sashes,** and **sword knots** instead of silver ones, and stamped white fittings to the epaulettes (218).

27 December 1812– The newly formed **Sapper Regiment** was ordered to have the exact same uniform as Pioneer regiments, but with a three-flamed grenade on the shako, and silver buttonhole lace on the collars and cuff flaps of officers' coats. Shoulder straps were red (Illus. 1708) (219).

29 December 1812– Sappers and pioneers were given **muskets** like those of dragoons in place of pistols (Illus. 1709) (220).

20 May 1814– The **gray campaign riding trousers** with buttons used by officers of Sapper and Pioneer regiments were replaced by similarly gray ones with black **double stripes** with red piping (both stripes and piping being of cloth), and without leather lining (221).

31 July 1814– **Pistols**, retained at this time only by miners, were withdrawn from them and replaced with dragoon muskets (222).

In 1814, it was ordered that the **cockades** on officers' hats have white tape around them, which was later replaced by silver. In 1815 the placement of **chevrons** sewn on drummers' coats was changed, these coats being from this time on single-breasted with small hooks instead of buttons, and with tape or lace on both sides of the opening, following the example, as stated above, of drummers of in the Army Infantry and Foot Artillery (223).

11 January 1816– With the separation of the Sapper and two Pioneer regiments into two Sapper and seven Pioneer battalions, lower ranks in all of these were ordered to have red **shoulder straps**. Pioneers were to have a small single-flame grenade [*grenadka*] on **shakos** and **pouches**, and sappers and miners were to have three-flame grenades (224).

24 January 1816– In all battalions **scabbards** for short swords [*tesaki*] and officers' swords [*shpagi*] were ordered to be black throughout the Foot Field Artillery, the first being polished, and the second lacquered (225).

27 January 1816 – The red **shako cords** used in these battalions were replaced by white ones, and Sapper officers were ordered to keep the **buttonhole lace** on their coats (226).

9 March 1816– Highest confirmation was given to a new authorization table of **uniforms, accounterments, and weaponry** for Sapper and Pioneer battalions, based on which all personnel in these battalions kept their previous uniforms and weapons with only the following small changes and additions:

1) **Shakos** were given that were taller than before, with a flat top that was no longer concave (Illus. 1710 and 1711).

2) Dark-green **pants** were prescribed for combatant lower ranks instead of white.   3) Apart from the battalion number on **shoulder straps** and **epaulettes**, it was ordered to also have the initial letters of the unit title, namely: in the 1st Sapper Battalion – Cyrillic 1 S.B., in the 7th Pioneer Battalion – Cyrillic 7 P.B., and so on. These numbers, as before, were of yellow cord for lower ranks and of silver cord for officers.

4) The **musicians** introduced in the tables of authorized personnel [*shtaty*] for all these battalions were prescribed the same uniform distinctions as these ranks had in the Army Infantry and Foot Artillery (Illus. 1710).   5) **Sword-knot tassels** in the first companies were designated to be white, in the second companies – orange, in the third – yellow, and in the fouth – sky blue.

6) In each sapper company (for use during practice and exercises), black **iron helmets and cuirasses** were authorized for one officer, one noncommissioned officer, and four sappers (Illus. 1712). For miners, in case of mining work during wartime, it was ordered that one **pistol** be held for each man (227).

13 April 1816 - Field and company-grade officers were ordered to wear cloth **pants** with high boots only during reviews and parades, and during the rest of the time to have the riding trousers with stripes prescribed in 1814, with the exception of officers in the capitals, where they were prescribed to be in dark-green pants and high boots (228).

23 May 1816 – Field and company-grade officers of Sapper and Pioneer battalions were given gorgets of the same pattern as in Army Infantry regiments (Illus. 1713) (229).

16 November 1816– All combatant ranks of these same battalions were ordered to have **red piping** all around the collar (230).

8 August 1817- The size of the **forage cap** was fixed as established at this time for forage caps in Army infantry regiments (231).

26 September 1817 – The description confirmed on this day of **shakos** and **accouterments** and the rules for wearing them were adopted in Sapper and Pioneer battalions. Along with this, it was ordered that shakos in Sapper battalions have the exact same plate as in Grenadier and Carabinier regiments, except made of white tin and with the addition of two crossed axes beneath (Illus. 1713 and 1714). Sapper companies of Pioneer battalions kept the previous small grenades with three flames (Illus. 1715), while Pioneer companies had them with one flame (Illus. 1716 and 1717). On pouches in Sapper battalions and the Sapper companies of Pioneer battalions the grenades remained with three flames, but in the Pioneer companies they had one flame, both kinds being of yellow brass (Illus. 1715 and 1717). The grenades on drummers' crossbelts followed those on the pouches in regard to the number of flames (Illus. 1718)(232).

8 December 1817- The leather **leggings** [kragi] on the cloth pants were ordered to have **integral spats** [kozyrki] of a pattern similar to the gaiter spats [shtibletnye kozyrki] of summer pants(233).

23 August 1818- Combatant lower ranks of Sapper and Pioneer battalions were ordered to have **shoulder straps** on coats and greatcoats that were as long as the shoulder and 2 1/8 inches wide, of the previous red color, with the battalion number 1 3/4 inches in size, cut out 7/8 inch from the lower edge of shoulder strap and backed with yellow cloth stiched around the edges of the cutout. The flaps or **wings** [klapany ili kryltsa] on musicians' and drummers' coats were prescribed to be of black cloth with red piping, while the tape for sewn-on trim, 7/8 inch wide, was white with a red stripe in Sapper battalions and all white in Pioneer battalions (Illus. 1718) (234).

22 January 1819– In all Sapper battalions it was ordered that the pompons or small plumes [repeiki ili kordonchiki] on privates' shakos be red, while in Pioneer battalions they were to be likewise red for privates in Sapper platoons but yellow for privates in Miner platoons (235).

25 January 1819- **Drumsticks** and **entrenching tool handles** in all Sapper and Pioneer battalions were directed to be yellow (236).

31 March 1819– In Sapper battalions lower ranks' **shoulder straps** were ordered to have the battalion number and the lettter C [Cyrillic S], while in Pioneer battalions the battalion number was accompanied by the letter _ (Cyrllic P). Colors were left as before, i.e. red shoulder straps with yellow numbers, letters, and periods (237).

12 October 1820- Field and company-grade officers of Sapper and Pioneer battalions were given a new pattern of **gorget** [znak], flatter and narrower than before, without a ribbon, of the same shape and with the same rank distinctions as were established in this year for field and company-grade officers of Grenadier, Infantry, and Jäger regiments (Illus. 1719) (238).

In this same year of 1820 there were changes in **musicians' and drummers' coats** when the chevrons on the sleeves began to be sewn on almost touching each other, and on the wings the tape was already not straight down to the lower edge, as before, but slanted; it also began to be sewn around all four edges of the collar (Illus. 1719). This style was also extended to the buglers introduced into Sapper and Pioneer battalions on 11 January 1820 (239).

17 January 1822– It was ordered that shakos in Army Sapper battalions have round **pompons** [pompony]: of red wool for lower ranks, silver for officers (Illus. 1720). Sapper platoons in Pioneer battalions were given the same pompons in red, but in yellow for Miner platoons (Illus. 1722). Along with this, all combatant lower ranks of Sapper and Pioneer battalions were directed to have red skirt **turnbacks**, with the skirt lining for officers also being red (240).

23 January 1822– In Pioneer battalions, it was ordered that there be two crossed axes under the grenade on the **shako** (Illus. 1721 and 1722)(241).

21 April 1822– The Sapper Battalion, being renamed from 1st Sapper Battalion, was ordered to have the letter C [Cyrillic S] on **epaulettes** and **shoulder straps**, without a number (242).

14 August 1823– The **9th Pioneer Battalion**, newly formed for the **Separate Lithuania Corps**, was ordered to have the same uniform as other Pioneer battalions except with the addition of black lapels trimmed with a red cloth edge, with red cuff flaps instead of dark green. The uniform had black cloth gaiters [shtiblety] instead of leggings [krag], and epaulettes and shoulder straps had the number 9 on them (Illus. 1723 and 1724). The collar, lapels, and cuffs of lower ranks were of cloth, but of velvet for officers. Besides these distinctions pioneers of this battalion had shakos with white pompons, which were not authorized for other pioneers (243).

19 September 1823– With the renaming of this battalion as the Lithuania Pioneer Battalion, it was ordered that epaulettes and shoulder straps have the Cyrillic letters L and P instead of the number 9 and the letter P (244).

24 November 1823– Following the example of the Lithuania Pioneer Battalion, white **pompons** were ordered for the shakos of Pioneer platoons in other Pioneer battalions (245).

26 November 1823– All **musicians** of Sapper and Pioneer battalions, even though they might not hold noncommissioned officer ranks, were ordered to have coats with silver galloon and noncommissioned officers' pompons on the shako. However, this was not extended to drummers who did not hold noncommissioned officer rank (246).

16 January 1824 - The following changes were ordered to be carried out in the uniforms and accouterments of combatant lower ranks:

1.) **Coattails**, which up to this had one covering the other, were to be cut so that their inner edges came together, and sewn together so they touched.

2.) The decorative end [*trinchik*] of the **shako cords**, which was to be level with the right shoulder, was to have another special loop of white cord attached to the button on the right shoulder strap, so that the shako cords stayed in place when the soldier moved about (Illus. 1725).

3.) The **cartridge pouch** was to be worn so that when the soldier bent his elbow, the distance between it and the line of the top edge of the pouch was equal to 5 1/4 inches [*3 vershka*].

4.) **Knapsack chest straps** were to be fitted so that they were between the fourth and fifth buttons of the coat, as counted from the collar.

5) On the **musket sling** [*ruzheinyi pogon*], opposite the cocking piece, there was to be a band of the same kind of leather as the sling, for stowing the firing cover [*ognivnyi chekhol*] when it needed to be taken off (247).

29 March 1825- For combatant lower ranks, for faultless service, there were established **stripes** [*nashivki*] to be sewn on the left sleeve: for 10 years service - one, for 15 years - two, for 20 years - three; one over the other, all of yellow tape (248).

XII – ARMY HORSE PIONEERS (*ARMEISKIE KONNO-PIONERY*)

2 August 1822– Privates of the **1st Horse-Pioneer Squadron** were ordered to have a single-breasted dark-green coat with black collar and cuffs, red piping, shoulder straps, skirt turnbacks, and lining, with white buttons and a yellow number 1 on the shoulder straps, dark-green pants with red double-stripes and piping and leather trim at the bottom, a shako with a yellow lower pompon [*repeek*] and pyramid-shaped upper pompon [*pompon piramidal'nyi*], with white shako cords and a grenadier-pattern plate on which were two crossed axes beneath the star, and above them a small grenade with a single flame. A saber, sword belt with frog for the bayonet scabbard, carbine with bayonet, pouch [*lyadunka*], pistols, and complete set of horse furniture—prescribed as that in use at the time by Army Horse Jägers, except that piping on the shabrack was red while the edging, monogram, and crown were yellow, the last two being trimmed with black cord (Illus. 1726 and 1727) (249).

Noncommissioned officers had the same distinctions in respect to private Horse Pioneers as used in other branches of Army Cavalry (Illus. 1728) (250).

Trumpeters' uniforms were distinguished by red swallows' wings on the shoulders and white chevrons with a red center stripe [*reika*], of the exact same appearance as had been established for trumpeters in other Army Cavalry branches (Illus. 1729) (251).

Officers, with uniforms of the same color scheme as for lower ranks, had two gilt crossed axes on the lids of their pouches with a flaming grenade beneath, a gold number 1 on the silver field of their epaulettes, silver mountings to their pouches, silver monograms and crowns on the shabrack, and silver galloon trim to the shabrack with red piping along the edges (Illus. 1730 and 1731). When not on duty they were allowed to be in undress coats [*vitse-mundiry*] with long skirts and in the same frock coats [*sertuki*] used by officers of Sapper battalions, except with white lining instead of red (252).

1 May 1824– For officers and lower ranks the elongated **pompons** on the shakos were replaced by round ones (Illus. 1732) (253).

29 March 1825- For combatant lower ranks, for faultless service, there were established **stripes** [*nashivki*] to be sewn on the left sleeve: for 10 years service - one, for 15 years - two, for 20 years - three; one over the other, all of yellow tape (254).

XIII – FIELD AND GARRISON ENGINEERS. (*POLEVYE I GARNIZONNYE INZHENERY.*)

9 April 1801- Lower ranks of the Corps of Engineers were ordered to cut off their **curls** [*pukli*] and have **queues** [*kosy*] only 7 inches long, tying them midway down the collar (225).

8 May 1801– Generals and field and company-grade officers of the **Corps of Engineers** were ordered to keep their previous white buttons but in other regards have the same uniforms as established on 13 May and 16 June of this year for generals and field-grade officers of the Artillery, i.e. dark-green coat with similarly colored cuff flaps and pocket flaps; collar, cuffs, and skirt turnbacks all of black cloth; piping along three sides of the collar, the cuff flaps, and skirt turnbacks; shoulder straps of red cloth; lining of black stamin; white small clothes and gloves; hat with embroidered buttonhole and a black plume; boots up to the knee, with silver spurs (Illus. 1733) (256).

27 March 1802– All **Engineer** ranks were prescribed the same uniforms as those used at this time in the Foot Artillery, except with white buttons and red skirt turnbacks and lining (Illus. 1734) (257).

9 March 1803– It was ordered that officers' coats in the Corps of Engineers have silver **embroidered buttonholes**, two on each side of the collar and three on each cuff flap. Also, starting in this year officers began to wear **hats** with high plumes and narrow buttonhole lace of silver galloon instead of the previous embroidered style (Illus. 1735) (258).

1 October 1806- The **warm coats** [*fufaiki*] authorized for lower ranks up to this time were discontinued (259).

2 December 1806- Lower ranks were ordered to cut their **hair** short; generals, though, and field and company-grade officers, were in this case allowed to proceed according to their personal wishes (260).

10 March 1807 - **Canes** were abolished for officers and noncommissioned officers, i.e. officer candidates [*yunkera*, from German *Junker*], draftsmen-artists [*konduktory*; historically, these men were more or less on a track to become commissioned officers – M.C.], clerks, wardens [*vakhtery*, from German *Wächter*], and ordnance personnel [*tseikhdinery*, from German *Zeugdiener*] (261).

31 January 1808– In place of their previous shoulder straps, generals and field and company-grade officers were given **epaulettes** of the pattern used at this time in the Army Infantry, except completely silver and lined with red cloth (Illus. 1736) (262).

4 April 1809- **Noncommissioned officers** were ordered to have **galloon** not on the lower and side edges of the collar as was the case up to this time, but on the upper and side edges (263).

8 June 1809- The plumage around the sides of **generals' hats** was discontinued and the former pattern of buttonhole was replaced with a new one made of four thick, twisted cords, of which the two middle ones were intertwined with each other as if in a plait (264). In this same year **powdering of hair** was completely abolished for Generals and officers, and they were allowed to wear **frock coats** when off duty. These frock coats were like those introduced at this time for the Army Artillery except with silver buttons and red lining (265).

23 January 1810– Confirmation was given to an authorization table for uniforms and accouterments for lower ranks of the Corps of Engineers, based on which they were prescribed:

Officer candidates and draftsmen-artists [*yunkera i konduktory*] – uniforms like those used at this time by combatant noncommissioned officers in Pioneer regiments, including the pioneer short sword [*tesak*] on a white sword belt over the shoulder, with a black loop on the sword knot [*chernaya gaechka u temlyaka*] (Illus. 1737).

Clerks, wardens, and ordnance personnel– uniforms like those used by noncombatant noncommissioned offices in Pioneer regiments, but with dark-green lining to the frock coat [*sertuk*] instead of black, and instead of high cloth caps, *kiver* shakos like those of *konduktor* draftsmen-artists except without cords and the grenade, but with a bow (cockade), buttonhole loop, button, and red tuft or pompon [*kist' ili repeek*] (Illus. 1738). The loop and ring of the sword knot were black.

Barbers– as clerks, wardens, and ordnance personnel but instead of shakos—the same headdress as in Pioneer regiments (266).

17 January 1811- Instead of the multicolored **cords** on their **shakos**, Engineer officer candidates and draftsmen-artists were ordered to have white ones with the tassels [*kisti*] having black and orange mixed together (267).

5 February 1811– Engineer field and company-grade officers were directed to wear dark-green **pants** on all occasions and never use white ones (268).

22 February 1811 – **Shako cords** for officer candidates and draftsmen-artists were ordered to be red instead of white, with multicolored tassels as before (269).

25 October 1811– Lower ranks of the Corps of Engineers were given a new pattern dark-green **forage cap** with a black band and red piping on top and around the edges of the band. In shape and form these caps were completely identical to the forage caps introduced on 23 September of this year in Army Infantry regiments (270).

3 November 1811- **Gloves** were abolished for lower ranks holding noncommissioned officer status in the Corps of Engineers (271).

1812– Lower ranks in the Corps of Engineers were ordered to have: **collars** lower than previously, closed by small hooks; **leggings** up to the knee, with nine buttons; **shakos** lower than before, with a greater spread or widening toward the top and indented sides (Illus. 1739). Officers were given collars of the same pattern as for lower ranks, with buttonhole lace as before (Illus. 1739) (272).

1814– When on campaign or engaged in construction work, Engineer officers were allowed to wear gray cloth **riding trousers** with black double stripes piped in red down the middle. **Hats** were ordered to have white tape around the cockade ribbon, this later being changed to silver (273).

24 January 1816- In the Corps of Engineers the **scabbards** for swords [*tesaki*] and officers' rapiers [*shpagi*], were ordered to be black, the former being polished and the latter – lacquered. In this same year the Corps began to wear **collars** with red piping not only along the top and sides, but also along the bottom edge, and dark-green **pants** replaced gray ones for officer candidates and draftsmen-artists (274).

4 July 1817– Engineer generals and field and company-grade officers, as well as the troops and *konduktor* draftsmen-artists, were given **single-breasted coats** in place of double-breasted, with nine buttons, red piping around the collar, cuffs, and cuff flaps, and down the front opening and along the lower edge of the coat to the skirts (Illus. 1740) (275).

26 September 1817– The description confirmed on this day of army infantry **shakos** and **accouterments** was extended to Engineer officer candidates and draftsmen-artists, who from this time began to wear white **shako cords** instead of red (Illus. 1741) (276).

8 December 1817- The leather **leggings** [*kragi*] on the cloth pants of officer candidates and draftsmen-artists were ordered to have **integral spats** [*kozyrki*] of a pattern similar to the gaiter spats [*shtibletnye kozyrki*] of summer pants (Illus. 1741)(277).

23 August 1818- Lower Engineer ranks were ordered to have **shoulder straps** on coats and greatcoats that were as long as the shoulder and 2 1/8 inches wide, of the previous red color (278).

1 January 1819 – With the separation of Engineers into **Field** and **Garrison**, the first of these were left with their previous uniforms, while Garrison officers were ordered to have a coat without buttonhole lace, with black lining, and epaulettes trimmed in silver with a black field (Illus. 1742) (279).

4 April 1819- The **spats** on the leggings established on 8 December 1817 were abolished (280).

22 September 1819– Generals on the Engineering establishment, when wearing engineer coats, were ordered to wear the **hat** "fore-and-aft" [*s-polya*], as were field and company-grade officers (Illus. 1743) (281).

16 January 1824 – Engineer draftsmen-artists were ordered to have the **skirts** on their **coats** sewn together, and a loop of white cord sewn to the decorative end [*trinchik*] of the **shako cords** and fastened to the button of the right shoulder strap, as related in detail above for Army Infantry and Artillery (282).

29 March 1825- For combatant lower ranks, for faultless service, there were established **stripes** [*nashivki*] to be sewn on the left sleeve: for 10 years service - one, for 15 years - two, for 20 years - three; one over the other, all of yellow tape (283).

XIV - MILITARY-LABOR BATTALIONS AND COMPANIES
(*VOENNO-RABOCHIE BATALIONY I ROTY*)

25 November 1807– Military laborers [*voennye rabochie*] drawn from members [*ratniki*] of the Land Militia [*Zemskaya Militsiya*] for construction work in fortresses were ordered to have the same uniforms as train personnel [*furleity*] in Infantry regiments, with every color of cloth being permitted, such as: dark or light green, dark blue, gray, and even plain peasant cloth, as long as it was not black (284).

2 May 1816 – Privates, or military laborers, of the **1st and 2nd Labor Battalions** established to work for the Moscow Commission for Construction [*Moskovskaya Kommissiya stroenii*] were ordered to wear: gray jackets of peasant cloth with covered buttons: pants, forage cap, and greatcoat of the same material; black cloth neckcloth; blackened boots (Illus. 1744). In addition, a sheepskin coat [*polushubok*] was authorized for winter, and for summer—a smock [*kitel'*] and pants of raven's-duck (285).

11 April 1817– The newly established **Military-Labor battalions** of the **Lines of Communications** administration were prescribed the following uniforms and weaponry:

Master craftsmen privates and laborers– dark-green single-breasted coat with black collar, cuffs, and shoulder straps, with piping (around the collar, cuffs, cuff flaps, and on the skirt turnbacks), the battalion number on the shoulder straps which were backed with light-green, and tin buttons. Winter pants were dark green with light green pipin and spats attached to the leggings, while summer pants were of Flemish linen. The shako had no cords, but its pompon was white with a black center; chinscales were of white tin, as was a badge [*armatura*] depicting two crossed spades. The greatcoat was gray with collar and shoulder straps as on the dress coat. A knife for cutting fascines [*fashinnyi nozh*], without a sword knot, had a black handle and scabbard with iron mountings. The black sword belt was lacquered and had a yellow brass buckle. The knapsack and water flask were as for infantry, with black straps (Illus. 1745).

Noncommissioned officers– everything as for privates, but with their rank's prescribed galloon of the same color as the buttons and their shako pompon (Illus. 1746).

Company drummers– everything as for privates, with only the addition of black swallow's nests with light green piping and chevrons of tape made from white thread. Drum hoops, drumsticks, straps, and crossbelt were black (Illus. 1747).

Battalion drummers– everything as for company drummers, with only the addition of noncommissioned-officer distinctions (Illus. 1747).

Officers– coat and pants of the same colors as prescribed for privates; boots of the pattern used by officers in the rest of the infantry; silver epaulettes; the same shako as for lower ranks but with silver cords and pompon; sword [*shpaga*] and sash the same as for other infantry officers (Illus. 1748).

Noncombatants– everything as for noncombatants in Sapper and Pioneer battalions, with just the lining of the shoulder straps being light green.

Besides the uniforms described here for wear when in formation, master craftsmen and laborers were prescribed **work clothing**: for summer – canvas jacket [*parusinnaya kurtka*] with covered buttons and pants [*bryuki*] of the same material (Illus. 1749); for winter – a knee-length sheepskin coat [*polushubok*], gray cap of peasant cloth with ear flaps of the same material and a leather rear piece; gray pants of Russian flannelette [*russkaya baika*]; white leather mittens with woolen inserts [*varegi*], and warm overshoes [*ken'gi*, from Finnish *kenkä*], later replaced by loose boots with high shanks.   Lower ranks were not issued with **forage caps**, but they were made from coats that had passed their wearout time and had light-green piping, with the company number on the band in yellow cord (286).

29 June 1818– With a change in the numbering of Military-Labor battalions whereby the first two numbers were assigned to the two battalions located in Moscow, the **shoulder straps** of the former 1st Battalion received No. 3 and those of the former 2nd Battalion—No. 4 (287).

21 August 1818– Laborer privates, master craftsmen noncommissioned officers, and drummers, as well as officers and noncombatants, of **Military-Labor companies** under the **Corps of Engineers** were ordered to have the same uniform as Military-Labor battalions under the Lines of Communications administration, with everything light green being changed to red and the silver field of officers' epaulettes changing to black cloth trimmed with silver galloon and with the company number in silver (Illus. 1751, 1752, and 1753) (288).

10 March 1819– All **Military-Labor battalions** were ordered to have the same uniform clothing, accouterments, weapons, and other items as the Lines of Communications battalions referred to above (289).

4 April 1819– The spats that were part of the **leggings** of lower ranks' winter pants were removed (290).

2 February 1820– The two **Military-Labor Companies Nos. 37 and 38**, established at the Tula Arms Factory and belonging to the Garrison Artillery branch (later, on 23 March 1822, transferred to the Engineer administration)), were prescribed the same uniforms and weaponry as the Engineer Military-Labor companies referred to above (291). In this same year the tape on **drummers' coats** in Military-Labor battalions and companies was ordered to be sewn on closer together than before, as related above regarding the uniforms of other troops (Illus. 1754) (292).

16 January 1824 - The following changes were ordered to be carried out in the uniforms and accouterments of combatant lower ranks:

1.) **Coattails**, which up to this time had one covering the other, were to be cut so that their inner edges came together, and sewn together so they touched.

2.) **Knapsack chest straps** were to be fitted so that they passed between the fourth and fifth buttons on the coat, as counted from the collar (Illus. 1755) (293).

29 March 1825- For combatant lower ranks, for faultless service, there were established **stripes** [*nashivki*] to be sewn on the left sleeve: for 10 years service - one, for 15 years - two, for 20 years - three; one over the other, all of yellow tape (294).

XV - HIS IMPERIAL MAJESTY's Suite for Quartermaster Affairs.
(*Svita EGO IMPERATORSKAGO VELICHESTVA po kvartirmeisterskoi chasti.*)

9 April 1801– Column leaders [*kolonnovozhatye*] of HIS IMPERIAL MAJESTY's Suite for Quartermaster Affairs were ordered to cut off their **curls** [*pukli*] and have **queues** [*kosy*] only 7 inches long, tying them midway down the collar (295). [Note by M.C. – "Column leaders" were cadets holding noncommissioned officer status in H.I.M.'s Suite for Quartermaster Affairs. The "suite for quartermaster affairs" itself was a precurser to a general staff.]

20 May 1801– Generals and field and company-grade officers were ordered to have a double-breasted dark-green **coat**, with a collar and slit cuffs both of black velvet. Red piping was along three sides of the collar and on the cuffs, and skirt turnbacks were also red, as was the coat lining. Buttons, aiguillette, and embroidery on the collar and cuffs were all gold

(Illus. 1756 and 1757). **Pants** were left as before—of white cloth or whitened deerskin. **Boots** reached to the knees and had silver spurs, while **hats**, **sashes**, and **swords** were prescribed to be the same as in the Army Infantry (Illus. 1756). **Column leaders** were given the same uniform but the coat lacked the embroidery and aiguillette; the hat had a black buttonhole loop but no plume. The sword belt was of whitened deerskin with a gilded buckle, and worn over the coat. A sword and sword knot were as for officers (Illus. 1758). All ranks had white **gloves** and **canes** (made from cane reeds) (296).

15 January 1802– It was ordered to have **black velvet piping** along the turnbacks of officer's coattails, and the collar, cuffs, and shoulder straps of column leaders' coats were to be made from black velveteen [*plis*], all three having red piping (297).

In 1804– High plumes and buttonhole loops of narrow gold galloon (instead of the previous embroidery kind) were introduced for generals' and officers' **hats** (Illus. 1759) (298).

2 December 1806– Column leaders were ordered to cut their **hair** short. However, Generals and field and company-grade officers, were in this case allowed to proceed according to their personal wishes (299).

10 March 1807 - **Canes** were abolished for officers and column leaders (300).

16 September 1807– Generals and field and company-grade officers were ordered to have a gold **epaulette** on the right shoulder of the coat, with rank distinctions as in other branches (Illus. 1760) (301).

12 November 1808– Generals and field and company-grade officers were allowed to use **dark-green pants** for everyday wear, an in this same year there were introduced for their use **English saddles** and dark-green **shabracks** and **holsters** with black velvet trim, gold galloon, red piping, and silver stars (Illus .1761). It was also permitted for these ranks to wear dark-green **frock coats** with the same colored cuffs, black velvet collar, piping on the edges of the collar and cuffs, red lining, and gilt buttons (302).

8 June 1809- The plumage around the sides of **generals' hats** was discontinued and the former pattern of buttonhole was replaced with a new one made of four thick, twisted cords, of which the two middle ones were intertwined with each other as if in a plait (303).

In 1810– Instead of short white **pants**, column leaders were ordered to have dark-green ones with leather leggings with seven brass buttons; instead of high **boots** with spurs driven in—short ones with screw-in spurs; instead of hats— *kiver* **shakos** of the pattern used at this time by noncommissioned officers in Grenadier regiments, except with white decorations and without a plume; instead of rapier swords [*shpagi*]—lancer **sabers** [*sabli*] with an officer's sword knot, and instead of white **sword belts** worn over the coat—black ones worn under the coat (Illus. 1762) For mounted service they were prescribed dark-green **shabracks** with black velveteen trim, three red lines of cloth piping, and monograms and crowns of black velveteen lined with black cord (Illus. 1762). They were authorized officer-pattern **greatcoats**, gray with a black velveteen collar with the edges piped in red cloth (Illus. 1762). In this same year the **plumes** on officers' hats were shortened (304).

1812– All ranks were ordered to have: **collars** lower than previously, closed by small hooks. When on campaign, Generals and officers were allowed to wear **gray riding trousers** with brass buttons (Illus. 1763). Column leaders were given new **shakos**, lower than before, with an indented top (Illus. 1763) (305).

20 May 1814– Generals and officers were ordered to wear riding trousers without buttons, with red double stripes with red piping in between (Illus. 1764) (306). In this same year the cockades on generals' and officers' hats were ordered to have white tape around them, this later being changed to silver (307).

24 January 1816– The previously unblackened **sword scabbards** of generals and officers were ordered to be black and lacquered (308).

10 July 1816– Instead of the double-breasted **coat**, all ranks were ordered to wear single-breasted ones with nine buttons and red cloth piping around the entire collar, on the cuffs, down the front, and on the pocket flaps. Instead of one **epaulette**, Generals and officers were to have two, keeping the **aiguillette**, and also wear the **hat** "fore-and-aft" [*s-polya*]. Along with these changes column leaders were given **cavalry pants** with red double stripes and leather leggings (Illus. 1766 and 1767) (310).

26 September 1817– The pattern for army infantry **shakos** confirmed on this day was also accepted for column leaders (Illus. 1767) (311).

21 May 1825– Field and company-grade officers and column leaders of HIS IMPERIAL MAJESTY's Suite for Quartermaster Affairs who belonged to the **Separate Lithuania Corps** or the Reserve Guards Corps subordinate to TSESAREVICH AND GRAND DUKE CONSTANTINE PAVLOVICH were ordered to have all red piping, cuff flaps, double stripes on pants, and trim on shabracks and saddle cloths changed from red to raspberry (Illus. 1768) (312).

XVI - TOPOGRAPHERS (*TOPOGRAFY*)

10 July 1816 – The **Haapaniemi Topographic Depot** [*Gaapan'emskoe Topograficheskoe Depo*], being like the quartermaster section under the control of the Chief of HIS IMPERIAL MAJESTY's Main Staff, was ordered to have the exact same uniforms as this section, but with yellow piping, cuff flaps, and double stripes on the pants instead of red. Officers were to dress as officers, and cadets as column leaders (Illus. 1769) (313).

7 May 1817– Instead of the previous double-breasted **coat**, these personnel were ordered to have a single-breasted one with nine buttons and yellow piping around the entire collar, on the cuffs, down the front, and on the pocket flaps. Instead of a single **epaulette**, officers were to wear two, retaining the **aiguillette**, and wear their **hats** "fore-and-aft" [*s polya*] (Illus. 1770) (314).

28 January 1822– The **Corps of Topographers** [*Korpus Topografov*], established as part of HIS IMPERIAL MAJESTY's Main Staff, was prescribed the same uniform as His Majesty's Suite except with blue [*svetlosinii*] piping, cuff flaps, and double stripes on the pants. Officers were to dress as officers of the Suite, and topographers as column leaders. With this, topographers had a sword knot with a black strap and tri-colored tassel: white, black, and orange (Illus. 1771 and 1772) (315).

NOTES

(184) Ibid., Vol. XXVI, pg. 609, No. 19,826.
(185) Ibid., Vol. XLIV, pg. 25, No. 20,201.
(186) Ibid., Vol. XLIV, pg. 28, No. 20,201.
(187) Ibid., pg. 53, No. 23,205.
(188) For the uniforms of combatant and noncombatant lower ranks see the table of 27 December 1803. The description of officers' uniforms is taken from information received from the Commissariat Department of the War Ministry and statements by contemporaries. For doctors, see PSZ, Vol. XLIV, pg. 29, No. 20,109.
(189) PSZ, Vol. XLIV, pg. 31, No. 22,197.
(190) Information received from the Commissariat Department of the War Ministry.
(191) PSZ, Vol. XXIX, pg. 201, No. 22,382.
(192) Information received from the Commissariat Department of the War Ministry.
(193) Information received from that place, and PSZ, Vol. XLIV, pg. 67, No. 22,727.
(194) Ibid., pg. 27, No. 22,740, and information received from the Commissariat Department of the War Ministry.
(195) PSZ, Vol. XLIV, Pt. II, pg. 67, No. 23,335.
(196) War Ministry's Chancellery Archive, in the collection of directives signed by the Sovereign, Book 156, pg. 627, and received from the Commissariat Department of the War Ministry
(197) Ditto.
(198) Archive of the War Ministry's Inspection Department, in material regarding a proposal of the Minister of War's, with drawings and descritions, entitled: the manner of wearing knapsacks and greatcoats, 1808, No. 13,786/654; evidence from contemporaries.
(199) PSZ, Vol. XLIV, pg. 67, No. 23,335.
(200) Ibid., Vol. , pg. 663, No. 23,345.
(201) Information received from the Commissariat Department of the War Ministry.
(202) PSZ, Vol. , pg. 781, No. 23,478, and a model headdress preserved by the Commissariat Department of the War Ministry.
(203) Information received from that Department.
(204) PSZ, Vol. , pg. 950, No. 23,625; information received from the Commissariat Department of the War Ministry, and an actual model knapsack preserved there.
(205) PSZ, Vol. , pg. 1006, No. 23,695.
(206) Ibid., Vol. XLIV, pg. 24, No. 23,914.
(207) Ibid., pg. 25, No. 23,992, and information received from the Commissariat Department of the War Ministry.
(208) Ibid., Vol. , pg. 1632, No. 24,019.
(209) Information received from the Commissariat Department of the War Ministry; statements from contemporaries, and hats and frock coats preserved up to now.
(210) PSZ, Vol. I, pg. 362, No. 24,376.
(211) Ibid., Vol. I, pg. 517, No. 24,488.
(212) Ibid., Vol. XLIV, pg. 25, No. 24,511.
(213) Ibid., pg. 27, No. 24,528.
(214) Information received from the Commissariat Department of the War Ministry.
(215) PSZ, Vol.. XLIV, Pg. 27, No.24,829.

(216) Information received from the Commissariat Department of the War Ministry.

(217) PSZ, Vol. XLIV, pg. 70, No. 24,991.

(218) Information received from the Commissariat Department of the War Ministry; model examples preserved there, and items in various Arsenals or held by private individuals.

(219) PSZ, Vol. II, pg. 488, No. 25,297; information received from the Commissariat Department of the War Ministry; Collection of Laws and Directives relating to the Military Administration, 1816, Pt. 1, pg. 81.

(220) PSZ, Vol. II, pg. 497, No. 25,307.

(221) Information received from the Commissariat Department of the War Ministry, and statements by contemporaries.

(222) PSZ, Vol., pg. 844, No. 25,627.

(223) Information received from the Commissariat Department of the War Ministry, and statements by contemporaries.

(224) HIGHEST confirmed listing of Sapper and Pioneer battalions, 11 January 1816.

(225) PSZ, Vol. XXIII, pg. 450, No. 26,095, and information received from the Commissariat Department of the War Ministry.

(226) Collection of Laws and Directives relating to the Military Administration, 1816, Bk. 1, pgs. 81 and 82.

(227) HIGHEST confirmed table of 9 March 1816 and information received from the Commissariat Department of the War Ministry

(228) HIGHEST resolution regarding a report by the chief of the War Ministry, 13 April 1814.

(229) PSZ, Vol. III, pg. 854, No. 26,281.

(230) Ibid., Vol. XLIV, pg. 16, No. 26,518.

(231) Ibid., pg. 104, No. 26,992, and information received from the Commissariat Department of the War Ministry.

(232) PSZ, Vol.. XLIV, pgs. 104-108, No. 26,840.

(233) Information received from the Commissariat Department of the War Ministry.

(234) PSZ, Vol. XLIV, pg. 121, No. 27,504, and information received from the Commissariat Department of the War Ministry.

(235) Ibid., pg. 116, No. 27,649.

(236) Ibid., pg. 108, No. 27,653.

(237) Ibid., pg. 116, No. 25,748.

(238) Information received from the Commissariat Department of the War Ministry.

(239) Information received from that same place.

(240) PSZ, Vol. XLIV, pg. 103, No. 28,874.

(241) Ibid., pg. 117, No. 28,883.

(242) Information received from the Commissariat Department of the War Ministry.

(243) Information received from that same place, and memorandum of HISIMPERIALHIGHNESSthe Inspector-General for Engineer Matters to the acting Chief of HIS IMPERIAL MAJESTY's Main Staff, 14 August 1823, No. 1345.

(244) Information received from the Commissariat Department of the War Ministry, and PSZ, Vol. VIII, pg. 1220, No. 29,612.

(245) PSZ, Vol. XLIV, pg. 117, No. 29,654.

(246) Ibid., pg. 122, No. 26,658.

(247) Order to the Separate Corps of Military Settlements, 16 January 1824, No. 22, and information received from the Commissariat Department of the War Ministry.

(248) PSZ, Vol. XL, pg. 188, No. 30,309.

(249) HIGHEST confirmed uniforms for the Army Horse-Pioneer Squadron, 6 July, preserved at the Commissariat Department of the Warm Ministry; PSZ, Vol. VIII, pgs. 581 and 582, No. 29,155, and Vol. XLIV, pg. 102, No. 28,992; insignia [armatura] of the Corps of Engineers, issued in 1822, and statements from contemporaries.

(250) Ditto.

(251) Ditto.

(252) Ditto.

(253) PSZ, Vol. XLIV, pg. 103, No. 29,888.

(254) PSZ, Vol. XL, pg. 188, No. 30,309.

(255) PSZ, Vol. XXVI, pg. 609, No. 19,826.

(256) PSZ, Vol. XLIV,, pg. 25, No. 19,861, and information received from the Commissariat Department of the War Ministry.

(257) Ibid., pg. 25, No. 20,201.

(258) Ibid., No. 20,658.

(259) Information received from the Commissariat Department of the War Ministry.

(260) PSZ, Vol. XXIX, pg. 201, No. 22,382.

(261) Information received from the Commissariat Department of the War Ministry.

(262) PSZ, Vol. XLIV, pg. 25, No. 22,797.

(263) Information received from the Commissariat Department of the War Ministry.

(264) PSZ, Vol. , pg. 1006, No. 2369.

(265) Information received from the Commissariat Department of the War Ministry; evidence from contemporaries, and hats and frocks preserved up to now.

(266) Collection of Laws and Directives relating to the Military Administration, 1819, Bk. 1, pgs. 315-330.

(267) PSZ, Vol. I, pg. 517, No. 24,488, and information received from the Commissariat Department of the War Ministry.

(268) PSZ, Vol. XLIV, pg. 25, No. 24,511.

(269) Ibid., pg. 27, No. 24,528, and information received from the Commissariat Department of the War Ministry.

(270) Information received from that Department.

(271) PSZ, Vol. XLIV, pg. 898, No. 24,848.

(272) Information received from the Commissariat Department of the War Ministry.

(273) Statements from contemporaries.

(274) Information received from the Commissariat Department of the War Ministry.

(275) PSZ, Vol. XLIV, pg. 116, No. 26,956.

(276) Information received from the Commissariat Department of the War Ministry.

(277) Information received from that same Department.

(278) PSZ, Vol. XLIV, pg. 121, No. 27,504, and information received from the Commissariat Department of the War Ministry.

(279) Ibid., Vol. VI, pg. 3, No. 27,617, § 4, and Vol. XLIV, pg. 137, No. 28,072.

(280) Order of the Chief of H.I.M.'s Main Staff, 4 April 1819, No. 21.

(281) PSZ, Vol. VI, pg. 346, No. 27,933.

(282) Order to the Separate Corps of Military Settlements, 16 January 1824, No. 22, and information received from the Commissariat Department of the War Ministry.

(283) PSZ, Vol. XL,, pg. 188, No. 30,309.

(284) Ibid., Vol. XXIX, pg. 1329, No. 22,696.

(285) Ibid., Vol. III, pg. 626, No. 26,252, § 7.

(286) Ibid., Vol. XXIV, pg. 187, No. 26,785, § 5; Vol. XVIII, pg. 324, No. 27,713, and contemporary drawings of the uniforms of these bat

(287) Ibid., Vol. V, pg. 361, No. 27,435.

(288) Ibid., V, pg. 518, § 9; Vol. XLIV, pg. 117, No. 28,072; Vol. XLIII, Pt. II, book of authorization tables, addendum to Section One, pgs. 99 and 324 [sic], Vol.. 27,713, and information received from the Commissariat Department of the War Ministry.

(289) Ibid., Vol. XLIII, Pt. II, book of authorization tables, addendum to Section One, pgs. 99 and 234 [sic – see Note 288], No. 27,713, and Vol. VI, pg. 385, No. 27,991, § 3.

(290) Order of the Chief of H.I.M.'s Main Staff, 4 April 1819, No. 21.

(291) PSZ, Vol. VII, pg. 40, No. 28,125, § 8.

(292) Information received from the Commissariat Department of the War Ministry.

(293) Order to the Separate Corps of Military Settlements, 16 January 1824, No. 22, and information received from the Commissariat Department of the War Ministry.

(294) PSZ, Vol. XL, pg. 188, No. 30,309.

(295) Ibid., Vol. XXVI, pg. 609, No. 19,826.

(296) Ibid., Vol. XLIV, pg. 29, No. 19,879; information received from the Commissariat Department of the War Ministry, and evidence from contemporaries.

(297) Information received from the Commissariat Department of the War Ministry.

(298) Ditto.

(299) PSZ, Vol. XXIX, pg. 201, No. 22,382.

(300) Information received from the Commissariat Department of the War Ministry.

(301) Ditto.

(302) Ditto.

(303) PSZ, Vol. , pg. 1006, No. 23,695.

(304) Information received from the Commissariat Department of the War Ministry, and evidence from contemporaries.

(305) Ditto.

(306) Ditto.

(307) Ditto.

(308) PSZ, Vol. II, pg. 450, No. 26,095, and information received from the Commissariat Department of the War Ministry.

(309) Information received from the Commissariat Department of the War Ministry.

(310) PSZ, Vol. XLIV, pg. 120, No. 26,838, § 3; information received from the Commissariat Department of the War Ministry; statements by contemporaries and contemporary drawings.

(311) Information taken from the files of the General Staff Department's Archive.

(312) PSZ, Vol. XLIV, pg. 137, No. 30,353.

(313) Information received from the Commissariat Department of the War Ministry.

(314) Ditto.

(315) PSZ, Vol. VIII, pg. 49, No. 28,901, §§ 19, 20, and 21.

РИСУНКИ
ОДЕЖДЫ и ВООРУЖЕНІЯ
РОССІЙСКИХЪ
ВОЙСКЪ
1801-1825.

PLATES LIST OF ILLUSTRATIONS

1739. Draftsman-Artist and Company-grade Officer. Corps of Engineers, 1812-1816.

1740. Field-grade Officer. Corps of Engineers, 1817-1825.

1741. Draftsman-Artist. Corps of Engineers, 1818-1819.

1742. Company-grade Officer. Garrison Engineers, 1819-1825.

1743. General. Corps of Engineers, 1819-1825.

1744. Private. Military-Labor Battalions, in Moscow, 1816-1817.

1745. Private. Military-Labor Battalions, 1817-1824.

1746. Noncommissioned Officer. Military-Labor Battalions, 1817-1824.

1747. Drummers. Military-Labor Battalions, 1817-1825.

1748. Company-grade Officer. Military-Labor Battalions, 1817-1825.

1749. Private. Military-Labor Battalions, 1817-1825.

1750. Private. Military-Labor Battalions, 1817-1825. (In winter work clothing.)

1751. Private and NCO. Military-Labor Companies of the Engineer Administration, 1818-1824.

1752. Drummer, Military-Labor Companies of the Engineer Administration, 1818-1820.

1753. Company-grade Officer. Military-Labor Companies of the Corps of Engineers, 1818-1825.

1754. Drummer. Military-Labor Companies of the Engineer Administration, 1820-1825.

1755. Private. Military-Labor Companies of the Engineer Administration, 1824-1825.

1756. General and Company-grade Officer. HIS IMPERIAL MAJESTY's Suite for Quartermaster Affairs, 1801.

1757. Officer's coat embroidery, .H.I.M.'s Suite for Quartermaster Affairs, established in 1801.

1758. Column Leader. H.I.M.'s Suite for Quartermaster Affairs, 1801.

1759. Company-grade Officer. H.I.M.'s Suite for Quartermaster Affairs, 1804-1807.

1760. Field and Company-grade Officers. H.I.M.'s Suite for Quartermaster Affairs, 1807-1808.

1761. Officer's shabrack and holsters, H.I.M.'s Suite for Quartermaster Affairs, established in 1808.

1762. Column Leaders. H.I.M.'s Suite for Quartermaster Affairs, 1810-1811.

1763. Company-grade Officer and Column Leader. H.I.M.'s Suite for Quartermaster Affairs, 1812-1814.

1764. Field-grade Officers. H.I.M.'s Suite for Quartermaster Affairs, 1814-1816.

1765. Column Leader and Company-grade Officer. H.I.M.'s Suite for Quartermaster Affairs, 1816-1817.

1766. Field-grade Officer. H.I.M.'s Suite for Quartermaster Affairs, 1817-1825.

1767. Column Leader. H.I.M.'s Suite for Quartermaster Affairs, 1817-1825.

1768. Company-grade Officer and Column Leader. Separate Lithuania Corps, 1825.

1769. Company-grade Officer and Cadet. Haapaniemi Topographic Corps, 1816-1817.

1770. Cadet and Company-grade Officer. Haapaniemi Topographic Corps, 1817-1819.

1771. Field-grade Officer. Corps of Topographers, 1822-1825.

1772. Topographer. 1822-1825.

Private and Battalion Drummer. Pioneer Regiment, 1802-1803

Company-grade Officer. Pioneer Regiment, 1802-1803

Miner and Pioneer. 1st Pioneer Regiment. 1803-1806

1700

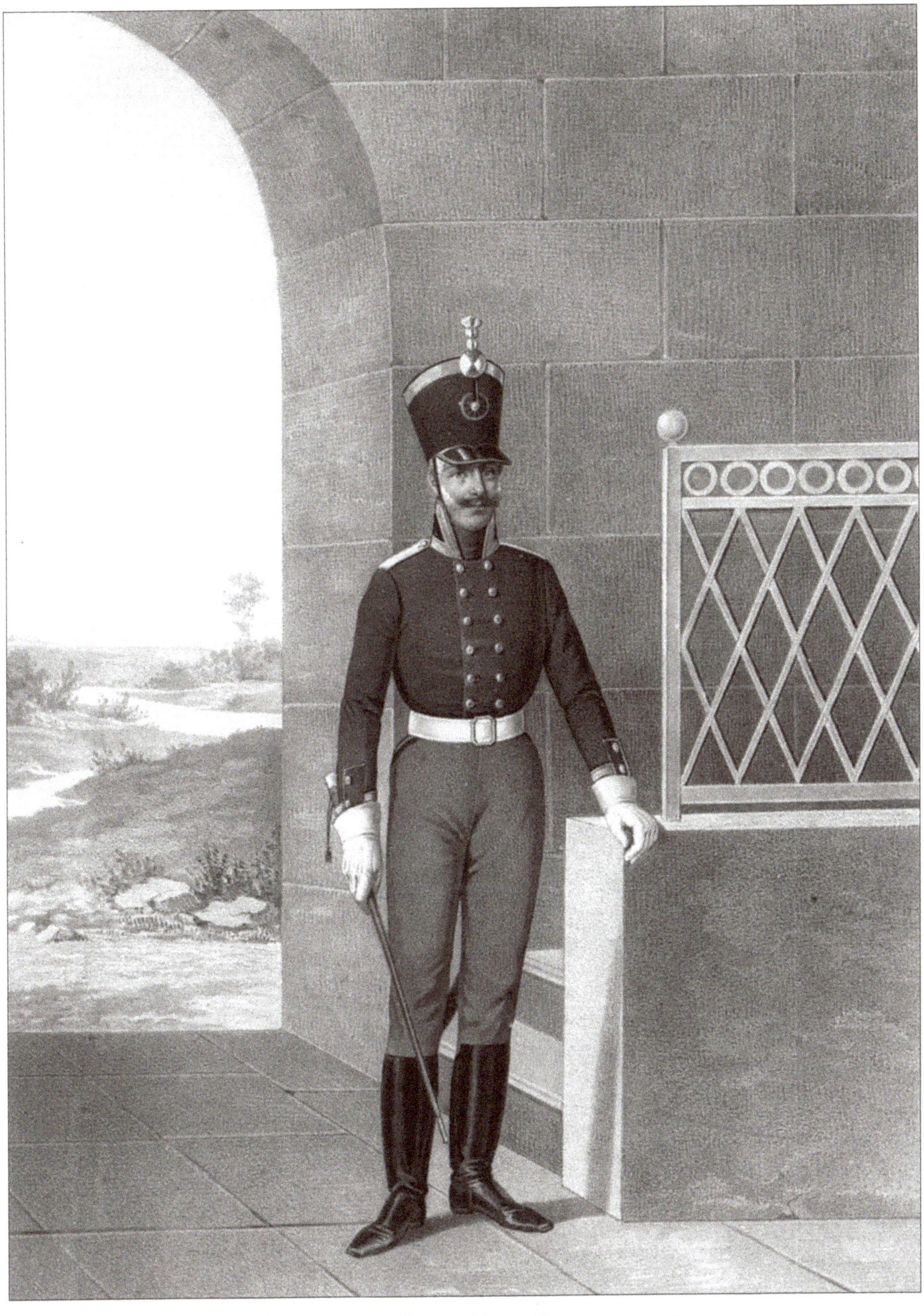

Noncommissioned Officer. 2nd Pioneer Regiment, 1804-1807

Drummer and Musician. 1st Pioneer Regiment, 1804-1807

Company-grade Officer and General. 2nd Pioneer Regiment, 1804-1807

Company-grade Officer and Pioneer. 1st Pioneer Regiment, 1808-1809

Noncommissioned Officer and Company-grade Officer. 2nd Pioneer Regiment, 1809-1810

Miner, Sapper, and Pioneer. 2nd Pioneer Regiment, 1809-1811

Company-grade Officer. 1st Pioneer Regiment, 1809-1811

Pioneer and Company-grade Officer. 1st Pioneer Regiment, 1812-1815

Company-grade Officer. Sapper Regiment, 1812-1815

Sapper and Pioneer. 2nd Pioneer Regiment, 1812

Musicians. Sapper and Pioneer Battalions, 1816-1817

Company-grade Officers. Sapper and Pioneer Battalions, 1816.

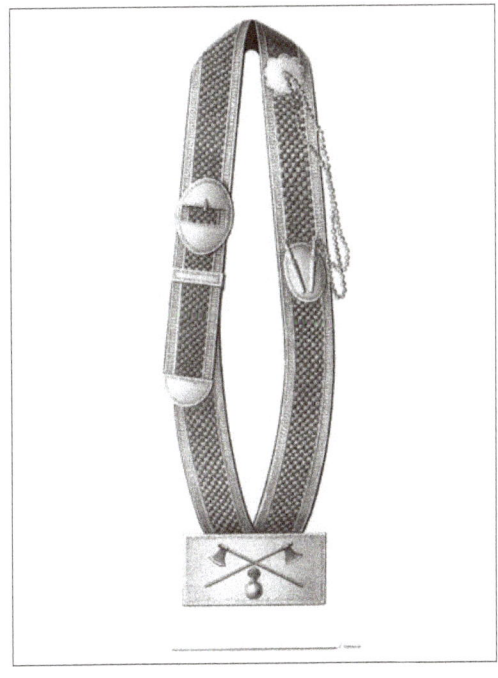

Sapper helmet and cuirass, established in 1816 - Shako Plate for Sapper Battalions, established 26 September 1817. (Note: Later, in 1818, 1819, or 1820, plates of this pattern were replaced by new ones of the style shown below in Plate No. 1705 [sic - should be 1719 and/or 1720 - M.C.]) - Shako plate of the 1st Horse-Pioneer Squadron, 1822-1828 - Officer's pouch, 1st Horse-Pioneer Squadron, established in 1822

1713

Field-grade Officer. Sapper Battalions, 1816-1820

Sappers. Pioneer Battalions, 1817-1821

Company-grade Officer. Pioneer Battalions, 1817-1820

. Pioneer. 1817-1825

Drummers. Sapper and Pioneer Battalions, 1817-1820

Bugler and Company-grade Officer. Sapper Battalions, 1820-21

Company-grade Officer. Sapper Battalions, 1822-1824

Sapper. Pioneer Battalions, 1822-1824

Miner Drummer. Pioneer Battalions, 1822-1825

Sapper. Lithuania Pioneer Battalion, 1823-1825

Company-grade Officer. Lithuania Pioneer Battalion, 1823-1825

Noncommissioned Officer. Pioneer Battalions, 1824-1825

Privates. 1st Horse-Pioneer Squadron, 1822-1824

Noncommissioned Officer. 1st Horse-Pioneer Squadron, 1822-1824

Trumpeter. 1st Horse-Pioneer Squadron, 1822-1824

Company-grade Officer. 1st Horse-Pioneer Squadron, 1822-1824

Noncommissioned Officer and Company-grade Officer. 1st Horse-Pioneer Squadron, 1824-1825

General. Corps of Engineers, 1801-1802

Company-grade Officer, Noncommissioned Officer, and Private. Corps of Engineers, 1802-1803

Company-grade Officer. Corps of Engineers, 1803-1807

Field-grade Officer. Corps of Engineers, 1810-1811

Draftsman-Artist [Konduktor]. Corps of Engineers, 1810-1811

Clerk. Corps of Engineers, 1810-1811

Draftsman-Artist and Company-grade Officer. Corps of Engineers, 1812-1816

Field-grade Officer. Corps of Engineers, 1817-1825

Draftsman-Artist. Corps of Engineers, 1818-1819

Company-grade Officer. Garrison Engineers, 1819-1825.

General. Corps of Engineers, 1819-1825.

Private. Military-Labor Battalions, in Moscow, 1816-1817.

Private. Military-Labor Battalions, 1817-1824.

Noncommissioned Officer. Military-Labor Battalions, 1817-1824.

Drummers. Military-Labor Battalions, 1817-1825.

Company-grade Officer. Military-Labor Battalions, 1817-1825.

Private. Military-Labor Battalions, 1817-1825.

Private. Military-Labor Battalions, 1817-1825. (In winter work clothing.)

Private and Noncommissioned Officers. Military-Labor Companies of the Engineer Administration, 1818-1824.

1752

Drummer, Military-Labor Companies of the Engineer Administration, 1818-1820.

Company-grade Officer. Military-Labor Companies of the Corps of Engineers, 1818-1825.

Drummer. Military-Labor Companies of the Engineer Administration, 1820-1825.

Private. Military-Labor Companies of the Engineer Administration, 1824-1825.

General and Company-grade Officer. His Imperial Majesty's Suite for Quartermaster Affairs, 1801.

Officer's coat embroidery, .H.I.M.'s Suite for Quartermaster Affairs, established in 1801.

Column Leader. H.I.M.'s Suite for Quartermaster Affairs, 1801.

Company-grade Officer. H.I.M.'s Suite for Quartermaster Affairs, 1804-1807.

Field and Company-grade Officers. H.I.M.'s Suite for Quartermaster Affairs, 1807-1808.

Officer's shabrack and holsters, H.I.M.'s Suite for Quartermaster Affairs, established in 1808.

Column Leaders. H.I.M.'s Suite for Quartermaster Affairs, 1810-1811.

Company-grade Officer and Column Leader. H.I.M.'s Suite for Quartermaster Affairs, 1812-1814.

Field-grade Officers. H.I.M.'s Suite for Quartermaster Affairs, 1814-1816.

Column Leader and Company-grade Officer. H.I.M.'s Suite for Quartermaster Affairs, 1816-1817.

Field-grade Officer. H.J.M.'s Suite for Quartermaster Affairs, 1817-1825.

Column Leader. H.I.M.'s Suite for Quartermaster Affairs, 1817-1825.

Company-grade Officer and Column Leader. Separate Lithuania Corps, 1825.

Company-grade Officer and Cadet. Haapaniemi Topographic Corps, 1816-1817.

1770

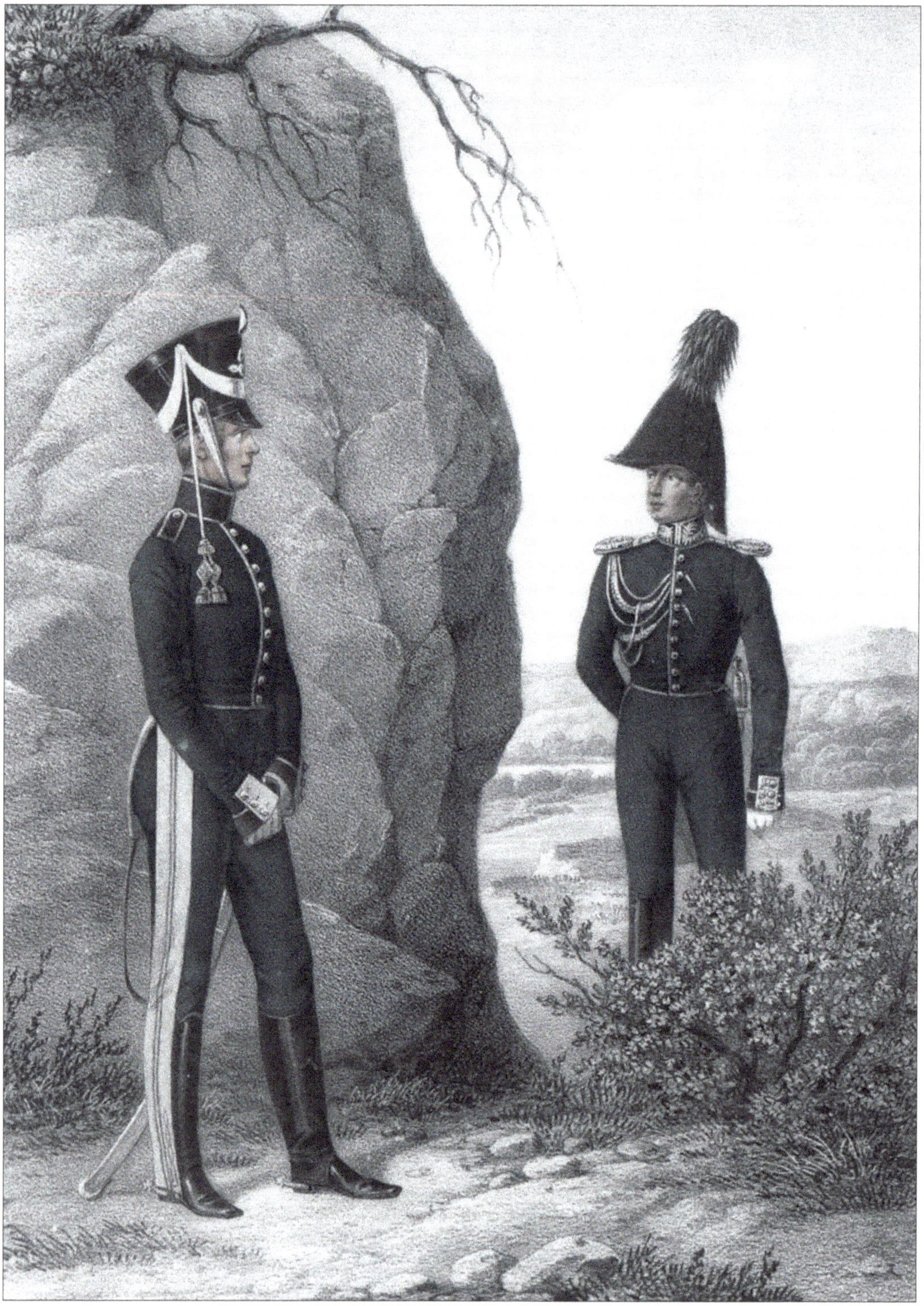

Cadet and Company-grade Officer. Haapaniemi Topographic Corps, 1817-1819.

Field-grade Officer. Corps of Topographers, 1822-1825.

Topographer. 1822-1825.

SOLDIERS, WEAPONS & UNIFORMS ALREADY PUBLISHED
(SEE WWW.SOLDIERSHOP.COM FOR ALL THE ISSUE)

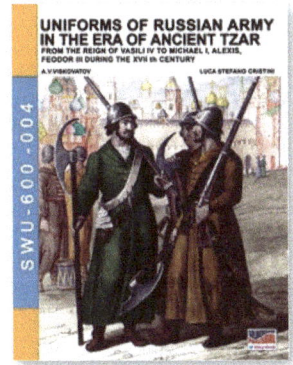

UNIFORMS OF RUSSIAN ARMY IN THE ERA OF ANCIENT TZAR
FROM THE REIGN OF VASILI IV TO MICHAEL I, ALEXIS, FEODOR III DURING THE XVII th CENTURY
A.V.VISKOVATOV   LUCA STEFANO CRISTINI
SWU-600-004

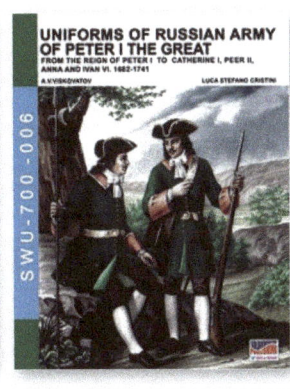

UNIFORMS OF RUSSIAN ARMY OF PETER I THE GREAT
FROM THE REIGN OF PETER I TO CATHERINE I, PEER II, ANNA AND IVAN VI. 1682-1741
A.V.VISKOVATOV   LUCA STEFANO CRISTINI
SWU-700-006

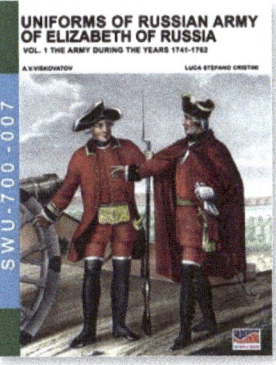

UNIFORMS OF RUSSIAN ARMY OF ELIZABETH OF RUSSIA
VOL. 1 THE ARMY DURING THE YEARS 1741-1762
A.V.VISKOVATOV   LUCA STEFANO CRISTINI
SWU-700-007

UNIFORMS OF RUSSIAN ARMY OF ELIZABETH OF RUSSIA
VOL. 2 THE ARMY DURING THE YEARS 1741-1762
A.V.VISKOVATOV   LUCA STEFANO CRISTINI
SWU-700-008

UNIFORMS OF RUSSIAN ARMY IN THE XVIII CENTURY VOL. 1
UNDER THE REIGN OF CATHERINE II EMPRESS OF RUSSIA BETWEEN 1762 AND 1796
A.V.VISKOVATOV - LUCA STEFANO CRISTINI
SWU-700-005

UNIFORMS OF RUSSIAN ARMY IN THE XVIII CENTURY VOL. 2
UNDER THE REIGN OF CATHERINE II EMPRESS OF RUSSIA BETWEEN 1762 AND 1796
A.V.VISKOVATOV - LUCA STEFANO CRISTINI
SWU-700-009

UNIFORMS OF RUSSIAN ARMY IN THE XVIII CENTURY VOL. 3
UNDER THE REIGN OF CATHERINE II EMPRESS OF RUSSIA BETWEEN 1762 AND 1796
A.V.VISKOVATOV - LUCA STEFANO CRISTINI
SWU-700-010

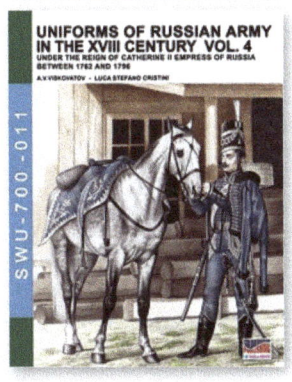

UNIFORMS OF RUSSIAN ARMY IN THE XVIII CENTURY VOL. 4
UNDER THE REIGN OF CATHERINE II EMPRESS OF RUSSIA BETWEEN 1762 AND 1796
A.V.VISKOVATOV - LUCA STEFANO CRISTINI
SWU-700-011

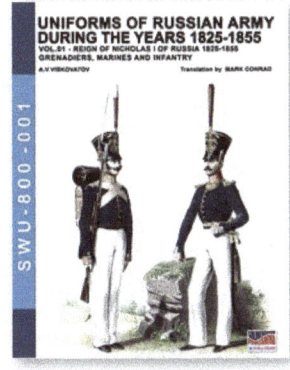

UNIFORMS OF RUSSIAN ARMY DURING THE YEARS 1825-1855
VOL.01 - REIGN OF NICHOLAS I OF RUSSIA 1825-1855
GRENADIERS, MARINES AND INFANTRY
A.V.VISKOVATOV   Translation by MARK CONRAD
SWU-800-001

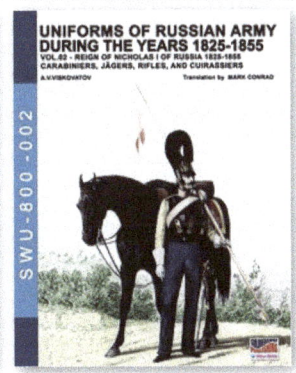

UNIFORMS OF RUSSIAN ARMY DURING THE YEARS 1825-1855
VOL.02 - REIGN OF NICHOLAS I OF RUSSIA 1825-1855
CARABINIERS, JÄGERS, RIFLES, AND CUIRASSIERS
A.V.VISKOVATOV   Translation by MARK CONRAD
SWU-800-002

UNIFORMS OF RUSSIAN ARMY DURING THE YEARS 1825-1855
VOL.03 - REIGN OF NICHOLAS I OF RUSSIA 1825-1855
DRAGOONS, HORSE-JAGERS, LANCERS & HUSSARS
A.V.VISKOVATOV   Translation by MARK CONRAD
SWU-800-003

UNIFORMS OF RUSSIAN ARMY DURING THE YEARS 1825-1855
VOL.04 - REIGN OF NICHOLAS I OF RUSSIA 1825-1855
GENDARMES, TRAIN, ARTILLERY, SAPPERS & PIONEERS
A.V.VISKOVATOV   Translation by MARK CONRAD
SWU-800-004

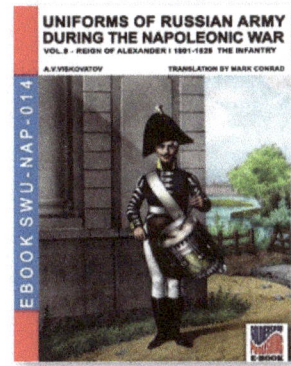

UNIFORMS OF RUSSIAN ARMY DURING THE NAPOLEONIC WAR
VOL.9 - REIGN OF ALEXANDER I 1801-1825 THE INFANTRY
A.V.VISKOVATOV   TRANSLATION by MARK CONRAD
EBOOK SWU-NAP-014

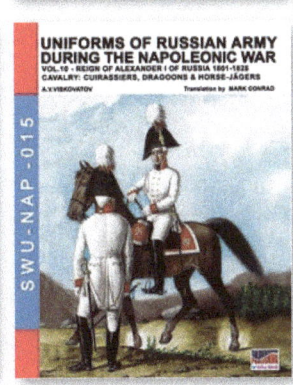

UNIFORMS OF RUSSIAN ARMY DURING THE NAPOLEONIC WAR
VOL.10 - REIGN OF ALEXANDER I OF RUSSIA 1801-1825
CAVALRY: CUIRASSIERS, DRAGOONS & HORSE-JÄGERS
A.V.VISKOVATOV   Translation by MARK CONRAD
SWU-NAP-015

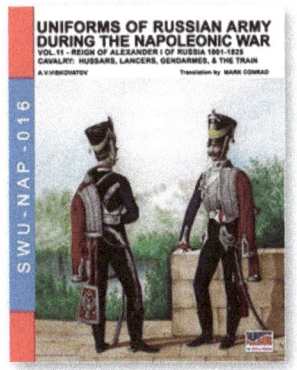

UNIFORMS OF RUSSIAN ARMY DURING THE NAPOLEONIC WAR
VOL.11 - REIGN OF ALEXANDER I OF RUSSIA 1801-1825
CAVALRY: HUSSARS, LANCERS, GENDARMES, & THE TRAIN
A.V.VISKOVATOV   Translation by MARK CONRAD
SWU-NAP-016

UNIFORMS OF RUSSIAN ARMY DURING THE NAPOLEONIC WAR
VOL.7 - REIGN OF PAUL I OF RUSSIA BETWEEN 1796 AND 1801
THE INFANTRY GRENADIERS, MUSKETEERS AND JÄGER
A.V.VISKOVATOV   Translation by MARK CONRAD
SWU-NAP-007